This book is dedicated to my kids who had to endure growing up listening to me talk to them like this every freaking day of their young lives.

I also dedicate this to the few individuals that also suffered as my captive audience due to being my work partners. I hope God has had mercy on them once they escaped!

And it's my sincere hope that a few people are able to find this book and the information within helps them navigate life a little better.

I make no pretense to being a wise man, despite the number of people who have said I am wise. I'm not a self help guru and I'm not some kind of academic genius. I really am an incredibly average guy.

The driving inspiration here is plain and simple. I was truly lucky or blessed to have a few men pass through my life that knew important information that I wanted and needed. They shared bits of wisdom and taught me critical skills. It's hard to image how much would have been missing in my life without those men. My grandpa had one hand. He taught me more through his self sufficiency than with words.

I also had some remarkable women that taught me things that the men never could. One inspiration was my grandmother. Gram taught me to cook when I was maybe 5 years old. She insisted that no grandson of hers was going to be helpless all his life, depending on someone to cook and clean for me, because there was no way to know if I would ever have to rely entirely upon myself due to unforeseen circumstances.

Whether you read this book or give it as a gift, THANK YOU!
And regardless of whatever age you might be when you read
it, I hope it's rather entertaining and that you find it helpful.

Why I Share This Information (Chapter 1)

Someone needs to.

I can't count the number of people who have
complained that public education did not prepare them
for real life as an unchaperoned adult.
I can't tell you how many times I've joked that my years
of schooling did not prepare me for the crazy twists and
turns of life.

There's a lot of things I've learned (mostly the hard way)
that have made me say out loud, "I wish someone
would have said something to me about this years ago."
So, I'm saying it.
Whether or not anyone listens, is not my choice.
I feel the need to speak. I just hope it helps someone.

So, that's my reason.
I'm hoping to be helpful to someone.
Everyone needs a reason. Most people call it a purpose.
Ya might say that my "purpose" for existing (and
sharing) is to be helpful.

There are books and classes devoted to "The Big
Questions."

Why do we exist?
Why do we do what we do?
What difference do we make?
What's the point?

This is not one of those books, because I ain't one of those people.
Many, many brilliant people have tried to answer these questions.
A few idiots, without being asked, have offered their own answers as well. Some people are serious and go on and on for hours about everything and nothing. Some folks attempt to be funny with answers like, "Well, there's chocolate and smooches."

I can't really answer the "Big Questions." Especially since I don't have a degree in 3 different mind game disciplines and a bunch of letters following my name from some elite university.
But, I can tell you with whole hearted conviction that everyone needs a little help and advice once in awhile. Everyone needs someone with experience and wisdom to tell them what to expect and what to worry about and what to not worry about. I think we can all appreciate someone we kind of respect when they tell us that we're doing ok and we have a reasonable shot at enjoying life.

Psychologist may be able tell you what may happen to someone that lacks a purpose or reason to go on living. They might even be able to explain why... to some degree.
I'm not a psychologist. I'm not a philosopher.
I'm really just your average Joe.

So, I don't have a long, elegant explanation.
I do have some simple, real world experience.

I once asked, "Why do people with no hope, go on living?"
No one could answer that for me.
But, I think I figured it out.
They live in the hope of finding hope.

People who have no hope, live in the hope of finding hope.

I hope I get a good job.
I hope I find the right mate.
I hope someday I understand.
I hope, I hope, I hope....

If someone speaks of suicidal thoughts, what do you (or people in general) do?
Most folks try to help them see a reason to live.
Some might give a reason not to die.
Ultimately, they're trying to give the person hope in something better that can't be seen yet.
There's a hope in finding hope. There's hope in finding a reason.

Now.... for the love of all that is holy and right...
IF someone you know is "in a dark place," do NOT hand them this book and tell them, "I hope this helps."

Dear God! That's not what this is all about! That's not what this book is about at all! I've already said that this book is all about stuff that I wish someone had said to me when I was younger. Please do not confuse my ramblings here about "finding a purpose"for myself in writing a book about information I find useful for some kind of intervention advice.

Disclaimer: I am an army veteran. (I know it's an odd transition, but it's the right time.) So, I'm gonna toss out a blanket apology for any dark humor that might find it's way into this book.
Maybe it's a surprise that I'm a veteran?
Maybe not. Maybe it's more of a surprise that I was once young and led a very different life.

You see, once upon a time, long ago, I was young.
At times it doesn't feel long ago.
At other times, it feels soooooooo looooonnnng ago.

Everyone has heard, "If I had known then what I know now..."
Almost everyone has said (and really meant) that.

What I really wish is that someone I respected would have taken me under their wing and said things to me that mattered. I needed someone with more life experience to point me in the direction of success on every level and in every arena.

Would I have listened? This is why I said "someone I respected."
I mean, seriously – why would I listen to anyone else?

Believe it or not, just because I was young and dumb, doesn't mean I was incapable of learning. It doesn't automatically result in refusing all wisdom. I was not hell bent to learn everything the hard way.

In fact, I realized early on that I didn't have to learn everything the hard way. Then, I figured out that I didn't have enough life to learn everything the hard way.

Case in point: a lot of cavemen and pioneers died figuring out which plants are safe to eat and smoke so that I could enjoy them with confidence and work on other things. I don't have to learn any of those basic survival fundamentals the hard way.

Someone learned the hard way how to control fire and electricity and other deadly things so I didn't have to learn the hard way. I could keep my eye brows and limbs and beating heart while enjoying the benefits of these things.

Naturally, I've learned more than a little the hard way. After all, I'm human.
Perfectly imperfect – tragically upbeat and happily downtrodden.
Thrilled with a life of magic and mystery while also perplexed to rage with a life of pain and disappointment.
I've even cried in the embrace of despair.
And I've hoisted the trophy of triumph that nearly cost me everything to attain.

Life is strange, even on the best of days.

This is probably the right time to finish explaining what makes me think writing this book was a good idea, and what makes me think I should be the one writing it.

My qualifications for writing this book:
1. I can read and write.
2. I survived my youth and adolescence to become old.
3. I've actually taken the time to think and learn and organize the things that I wish someone had said to me when I was younger.
4. I've actually had some really good mentors in my life.

That's it.
So, if you're looking for an ivy league professor or mountain top guru, I ain't it.
I'm a veteran and the son of a Vietnam veteran.
I'm the grandson of coal miners and railroad workers.
I've been to college.
I've lived, loved, lost and nearly died a couple times.
I've been married and divorced. I've raised children, and yes, I did change diapers and get up for 3 a.m. feedings.

I'm just a man, not a hero.
There's absolutely nothing amazing about me.

So what makes me think I should write this book?

Because every single person, at some point in life, will probably wonder why no one explained important ideas to them. I don't know everything, but I can explain a few important things. And I can do it in a rather simple way that can make sense.

As parents we're just kids learning to raise kids.
We turn to our parents for advice and wisdom more than we want to admit. We don't know everything and

it's when we become parents we learn just how much we DON'T know.

As kids, we know very little. But we want to learn.
As teens, we know everything, while adults are idiots stuck in the past and practically dying as we watch. Then, around mid-20-something – the tables turn and we realize we don't know everything and need help. By then, it might be too late. Or it's super hard to change.

So, here I am.
Writing. Hoping to be helpful. Praying to be useful and correct. I've lived long enough to know stuff.
And I believe that knowing things is important.

Example:

I was asked to help tutor 3rd graders with math.
One particular young man was failing.
Before talking math, I asked him what he wanted to be when he grew up.
He was adamant about being S.W.A.T.
OK. So, I asked how much he wanted to be paid.
His reply of $10/hr was perfect.
Let's do the math – short version:
$10/hr for 40 hour per week = $400
Taxes will take just under 25%, but let's just go with 25% for simplicity. That's $100/week the government takes.
"That's not fair!" he shouted.
I assured him that he was correct and we talked about that.
To continue:
I asked him how he would know if his employer was taking out the correct amount.

He didn't know.

I explained that if he didn't bother learning the simple math necessary to understand how much money the taxes would be, his boss could take out 30%, keep that extra 5% for himself and the young man would never know it.

Again he shouted, "That's not fair!"

I told him, "You are correct. But, you will never know if someone is lying to you and cheating you because you don't know how to do the math. You can't prove anything, because you can't do the math, so, they win."

We went on to work on basic math and he was able to catch up to his classmates in a very short time. That summer, he stopped me at the park to thank me because he was getting straight A's.

A couple years later, he stopped me again to thank me once more, because he was able to apply that moment we spent together in the 3rd grade hallway learning a reason to learn math to other areas of his life. He felt like he had been set on a pathway towards success in life instead of failing math.

All he needed was a reason.

The single most important thing to know early in life is that it's important to know things.

"Math is dumb."

Of course it is. Figure it out.

"Public school never taught me to do taxes."

In a round about way, they did. It's called math. If you learn math, you'll have a good base for figuring it out.

(Although, understanding "government speak" is a whole different language, and the government intentionally complicates the entire tax thing for their advantage. But, that's a long rabbit trail.)

But for real:
Knowing things is important.
Knowing how to know things is super important.

When we're born, we are wired and geared to learn. That's our job. It's also our hobby.
As we learn that we can learn, we want to learn more and more. We get into EVERYTHING because that's how we learn.

From birth, till we are sent to school, I believe we learn more in those few years than we will learn in most of our academic career. Do I really need to spell out how you couldn't even wipe your own butt? Yet by kindergarten, you could walk, talk, feed yourself and had learned or mastered a ridiculous load of other fundamental things necessary for you to live the rest of your life.

Those first 5 years of a child's life are the most important, monumental and critical. You are granted a human with no abilities beyond sleeping, eating and pooping. Eating isn't even really eating. It's sucking. And the only method of communication is crying. You'll learn all about that because they will teach you.

You have the insane task disguised as opportunity and obligation to teach them EVERYTHING in 5 years before they go to public school. You will teach them to walk, talk, brush teeth, eat, sleep and communicate. They will be looking to you for why. Why brush teeth? Why go to sleep? Why? Why? Why?

They will act like you know things and ask you about everything. They will act like you. They will take everything about you and amplify it and hand it back to you. You will have to teach and explain things you never thought about because once you learned it at age 2, you never thought about it again. Once you learned it, it became like breathing. You just do it without thinking about it.

You will not believe that you have to explain why your phone doesn't need a bath in the toilet. You will have to teach and explain why we don't run out into the road. In 5 years, you are taking a blob of a human that has no skills, knowledge or experience and crafting a semi-functional human. This is why parents of young children are so exhausted. And people will refer to these years of your child's life as "precious moments."

No one told me this!
Maybe I shouldn't tell you.
But, now you know.
Or at least, you've been warned.
And that is my reason for writing this.

How important is knowing stuff? (Chapter 2)

Well, let's do this real story:

Stephanie grew up in farm country.

She went to Moody Bible Institute in inner city Chicago. She took a class of big city kids on a field trip to farm country so they could see where their food is raised and how it gets to them.

The kids saw corn and beans and other vegetables growing in dirt.

They saw farm animals doing what farm animals do. And they saw how farmers milk cows and feed chickens. Then the kids went back home to the city.

The next day a very angry woman came at her. The woman was yelling at her and calling her names for "lying to the children about where milk comes from when everyone knows they make it at a processing plant."

Stephanie was speechless. Flabbergasted.

Where do you begin with that?

There really was a grown woman, in America, that didn't know that milk comes from cows. And she was serious about "correcting" the person that had grown up milking cows.

Is it important to know where milk comes from?

If you're the one getting the milk from the source, I'd say it's critical to know that you need to milk the cow and not the bull.

If you're just going to the store, maybe it's more important to know the difference between whole and skim and cream and whether you're lactose intolerant. But, I'm just sayin, it's probably good information to have – milk comes from cows – since there's a lot of people who depend on the people that milk the cows. I won't even address goat milk here.

How important is it to know stuff?
Ask any full time mechanic how important it is to know about replacing struts and how that spring works. If you know, you know. If you don't, just know that ignorance of the tools and power and delicate nature of the project can result in loss of fingers, toes, parts of your face... or it could kill you.

Chainsaws – knowing how to sharpen the teeth is important. Knowing when to run while felling a tree is incredibly more important. Knowing how to NOT get hurt while using a chainsaw is, in my opinion, infinitely important.

Lawn mowers – It's a little like the chainsaw thing. Proper maintenance and oil will allow you use the machine for many years so that you don't have to buy a new one. If you don't know proper maintenance, these expensive machines become expendable. Knowing how to maintain machines you use is very important for a few reasons beyond safety such as saving money.

Washing machine – yes, there's instructions on the machine and the detergent. Did you know that there's things you should know that are NOT in those instructions? Will you die if you don't know the things not written in the instructions? Most likely not. But, the chance is never 0%. (For example: electricity + water = bad. *At lease in certain situations.* This is not always in the instructions because it's supposed to be common knowledge. But, the machine uses both water and electricity.)

Reading, writing and language – it would seem very

difficult to live in a society where communication is literally everywhere if you do not possess this skill set of knowledge. Everyone loves to point out that the key to a successful and happy relationship/marriage is communication. That alone would seem to be a good reason to learn how to communicate in all ways to a high degree.

Camping – a little knowledge could be the difference between having a great experience with wonderful memories or being eaten by a bear. Or it could be worse, like wiping your bung hole with poison ivy.

The list of reasons and examples on why knowing stuff is important is infinite. Knowing stuff is literally the most important part of living (aside from breathing and other autonomic nervous system functions).

Let's look at this from the other angle.
What is the cost of NOT knowing stuff?

If you don't know how to change a flat tire, what are your options when it happens? Every car comes equipped with a spare and tools. You just need to know how to do it.

If you don't know how to sharpen a knife, you will periodically need new ones. Sharp knives cut easily, requiring less force. In turn, this reduces the chance of slipping off of whatever is being cut. A sharp knife that cuts easily is considered safer to use for this reason. Bonus: knowing the difference between a smooth and serrated blade and what they are each intended for can make kitchen work easier and quicker, which is more enjoyable.

If you don't know how and when to check the oil in your car, you can ruin your car.
Not knowing how to put air in your tires can be a serious problem.
If you don't know how to drive in snow, rain, mountain terrain – you probably need to avoid those conditions or rely on someone else.
If you don't know how to use the bus or rail system, you might have a very long walk.

If you don't know how to fix things in your house, it can be very expensive. If you don't know when to hire someone to fix something, it can be much more expensive because you might let it get worse than it should have been. And if you try to fix it, but don't know how, it can be super expensive when you botch it.
If you don't know about smoke detectors and CO detectors and emergency escape routes and fire extinguishers and electrical hazards and what to do in event of a water leak, it would seem to be less than ideal - maybe even not safe.

Let's say you spawn.
Is there any argument about how important it is to know how to keep your child alive?
Do you know correct foods for different ages?
How about safety around the house?
Car seats? What if they get sick? Do you know what to do? What happens if you don't?

What about your own health?
How bad would your teeth be if you didn't know to

clean them?

What if you didn't know about penicillin when you need it?

How do know when to go to the doctor and when to ride it out?

Would you be ok if you didn't know about sleep and diet and exercise?

Let me be a bit more extreme so as to be clear:

Would you put complete trust and faith in the hands of someone next to you that was mixing explosives if there was any doubt about their knowledge in what they were doing?

Would you feel safe in the bus being driven by someone that has never driven anything before and has no knowledge of the city streets? Would you eat puffer fish being prepared by someone at his backyard BBQ after watching a Japanese chef prepare one on YouTube? (If you didn't know, it can be deadly if not prepared correctly.)

They say ignorance is bliss.

I suppose that's because you can't care about something you know nothing about.

If you don't know how much of your money the government wastes, you don't care. It doesn't bother you. ("Can't do anything about it" is a different discussion.)

If you don't know your significant other is cheating, you don't care. After all, how could you care when you don't know?

How important did it just become to you to be able to know stuff?

And how important did it become to know how to know?

So, that's why I've written this book. I know stuff. Sure, some of it may be obsolete before anyone reads it. Kinda like jaz drives showed up for computers and were gone before hardly anyone bought one. Oh? Never heard of a jaz drive for computers? That's the point. It existed. Then, in a very short time it was obsolete.

But, a lot of things I've learned are fairly universal and common to all people.

BTW: this is not a book of advice.
It's not a parenting book.
It's not a map or a guide or a magic remedy for anything.

So, what's the point?

Simple. Information.

There are things I wish were said to me.
Had I heard them, I might have embraced and believed them.
If I had... oh, how much better life could have been!

So, I'm saying those things.
Whether anyone listens or believes me is up to them.
I'm just offering information.
Believe it or burn it down.
I've lived my life.
But, if the things I've learned can be useful, I kinda feel like I'd be selfish to never say anything.

Mortality is real. (Chapter 3)

They say, "You can't take it with you."

Bullshit.

Money, cars and physical goods will certainly remain on earth and in use after I'm dead. And those things will no longer belong to me. They will be claimed by someone else.

However, everything I am, every thought I've ever thought, every idea I've ever come up with... these things will go with me. My memories will be buried with me. The experiences I've cherished will only exist in the past of my existence. All the moments I've loved and celebrated and lamented and endured will cease to exist the moment my brain shuts down. No one – even the kids I've raised – will ever know what it's like to live life as I have.
My personality will be in the ground with me.
Every single everything that makes me ME will not exist without me.
When I die, I take all that with me.
All my feelings go with me.
I will take all of me with me.

Some will argue that as long as the things I've written down are in print, part of me will live on. Perhaps. But, books get burned and banned and deteriorate. Or no one ever reads them. I can't really argue the point. I simply believe that when I die, all of what I am, think, feel, believe and have experienced goes with me. To some extent, my memory (meaning that I am remembered) will live in the hearts and minds of my family and a few friends. But, that will only last a little while.

Walk through any graveyard.

There's a lot of graves. But, those are only the ones that were buried.

The ones cremated, or the ones buried in shallow graves with no markers, or those buried in mass graves and all those buried at sea have no stone testament to their existence.

As you look at the gravestones, you only see names and dates. Maybe there's a quote. Maybe there's an image or some short summary of their life. Any idea who they were? Or why they mattered?

Their life ended and was loaded into a coffin and buried with a (mostly) permanent stone marker. Their name, birth date and date of death are all we have of them. That seems like an odd summary of their life.

It's like the only thing that mattered about them was that they existed and were identified, then died.

A super sad reality is that no one younger than you has experienced what you have experienced. Because of that, they don't care about all the obsolete tech and information you have lived.

I have never truly understood what it would feel like to see a car for the very first time in history. I couldn't imagine the experience of what it might have been like to cross a thousand miles of prairie and desert just to find out there's this insane hole called the Grand

Canyon that no one knew was there. I grew up with TV, so I couldn't know what it was like to experience the first time someone in my neighborhood got the first one in our neighborhood. My parents tell me what it was like, but I wasn't there. I never understood what it meant for my parents to know where they were and what they were doing when JFK was assassinated... until 9-11. I remember vividly that I had just dropped my son off at preschool and rushed home to turn on the TV and watch the 2nd plane hit. I hope my kids NEVER have that kind of moment in their life, but somehow... I know they will.

Maybe we've reached a point in history where technology is so intuitive and people have grown so familiar with it that younger generations will never experience the trauma of programming a VCR. Perhaps humans in the 1st world countries will never know what it's like to have new technology come along that baffles them. It's possible that anything invented or introduced from here on out will "just work" and kids will not grow up to be seen as "tech-idiots" by younger kids. My grandchildren may not need their grandchildren to help them with computers and gadgets and gizmos.

For those of us who are older:
My grandparents were born into a world where horses were still the main mode of transportation.
My parents were born into a world where air travel was limited to the military and the wealthy.
I was born into a world that was rapidly evolving into the computer age and only the wealthy had cell phones.
My kids were born into a world connected by easy

travel and digital communication where everyone has a smart phone. We have the world in the palm of our hand, and they've never really known anything else. My granddaughter has come into the world when technology is building new technology and replacing the need for humans.

When my grandparents passed, they took those experiences with them. I can only read about what they lived through. I can't hear them tell those feelings anymore. I can't see their eyes well up as they relive the Great Depression. I will never feel their joys and sorrows and regrets and victories of survival because they can't tell me those things in person. It all went with them.

When my parents pass, I will have a few super 8 movies and video cassette memories of them. There may be a bunch of cell phone videos, but only in their later lives. Most of what they lived, will cease to exist just like when their parents passed.

When I die, my kids will have a few video cassette memories and much more cell phone footage of me. And there will be more and more video footage of my kids for their kids. And there will be much more video information of my grand kids.
Will this convey more feelings? Will they experience more of the generational wealth of knowledge? I don't know. I'm not sure anyone can know.

I do know, that while I can relive some feelings because of a smell or a song, those feelings and memories will go with me when I leave this planet.

Life Is (Chapter 4)

Life is a horrible trap.
But, only if you allow it to be so.
Life is the gift of a lifetime.
But, only if you claim it.

Loneliness is a misery that will drive you mad.
It's a terrible cycle to get into. When we get lonely, we
don't want to be lonely. The problem is that we tend to
try to latch onto someone hoping they can drag us out.
We're hoping someone can pull us out of the loneliness.
But, they panic and shake us off. We see them reject us
and we get more lonely and desperate. Loneliness can
be seen and felt by others. And no one wants to get
sucked into it.

The irony to loneliness is that in order to get away from
it or stay away from it, we can't appear lonely. We have
to figure out a way to be "not lonely" in order to not be
lonely.
I know. It makes no real sense, but yet, we know that's
really the way it is.

Think of it like this:
Would you rather be around someone lonely and
depressed
or
someone that's positive with their shit together?
Exactly.

Love is the sweetest and most miserable gift of life.

And there's no denying that it's a huge part of life.
Once you've been loved and in love, you'll understand that statement.
We need it, want it, and love it.
Then, it tears us apart and drops us to our knees.
It sends us on a magical fantasy and trips us.
They say "love is blind," but I've come to believe that it makes a person see things in someone that I absolutely do not see. It can makes us do things and believe things we would have never come up with on our own.
Love is a task master that cares beyond believe.
It's an ogre with a heart of gold.
If all this sounds confusing and crazy, you got it!
That's exactly what love is like.

Love is impossible to describe.
That's why there's infinite songs and books and studies on it.
It's like no one knows what it really is.
Even the ancient Greeks had 7 different words for love.

But, I think I have a solid answer.

Love is a decision.
That decision becomes an infinite string of decisions.
Love is a choice that continues to choose.
No one is perfect. Obviously.
So, we make the decision to talk. We choose to communicate. We decide to work on communication, wants and needs. We choose to put each other first. We decide to care, even when it's getting rough. We choose to listen and understand. We decide to forgive, give, encourage, and make things better. And the cycle goes on forever.

Some folks might try to describe it with the fruits of the spirit:
Love, Joy, Peace, Patience, Kindness, Generosity, Faithfulness, Gentleness and Self Control.
Well – love is actually IN the list. Soooo....

What I see is a list of choices.
I don't see a single thing here that can't be shared with someone.
In fact, they can't be gifts if you don't share them.
And I don't see any of these happening unless you decide.
I actually see these as gifts of YOUR spirit that you have to give... not so much as gifts you receive from the spirit. I'd say that we are given these gifts to give as gifts.
(Dear theologians: I went to seminary. I already know your apologetics. I understand and actually believe it goes both ways: give and receive. It's ok if you don't agree.)

I may not have THE answer to what love is, but I believe this answer to be solid.

You have heard the remark that you shouldn't take life so seriously, because none of us will get out alive. It's a funny saying, but true.
It also has a certain amount of reasoning that can be applied to many situations.
For example: You were head over heels in love. They left you. You feel like your world is over. This is when you should remember that your life on this rock is limited and you don't have time to feel this bad for long. Mourn

the loss of love. Cry. Get it out and get over it. Use the rest of your time to learn from what you survived and do better. Make the most of the time you have left on earth.

Oh, wait.
That sounds kinda cold? That sounds like I don't understand or care?
Do you REALLY believe I haven't been there and learned from it? Really?
Why do you think I'm writing this?
You're unique, yes, but your situation isn't.
Your love isn't.
Let's put it like this: If your love was so special... so unique... so different... how did you end up in the exact same position as almost everyone else before you?

Life is the best and worst place I've ever lived.

You're gonna love and lose.
Learn and do better.
I beg you.

This World Will Change (Chapter 5)

Clearly the world is crazy.
To think otherwise is just nuts.
Clearly the world has changed. It always has.
Any 3rd grader that's seen a 10 minute film about history can tell you that the world has changed. Anyone that's taken even one history class can tell you that the world has always been changing since the very beginning. The

world has changed. That's never changed. And it will continue to change. That will never change. From single cells to dinosaurs, to hat styles over the ages, everything always changes.

So, at this point in human history, in the United States, in the year 2023, some of this material will no longer matter in 6 months or in a year. But, as far as our lifetimes go, most of this will remain true.

After all, despite all of the change, some things never really change.
At least not in our lifetimes. There's an idea that humans will no longer have toes some day because of wearing shoes.... Maybe. But, definitely not in my life time, my kids, my grandchildren or even my 3X great grandchildren.

Governments change, but no they don't.
They don't look the same, but they behave the same. Dictators come and go. They're all different, but really the same.
Education changes, but it's still teaching.
Normal people in civilization have to work for value that's exchanged for survival. Animals behave like animals. Some things do not change.

It's a weird 2 am dorm room conversation about how everything changes but nothing really changes. What more can I say? The folly of it becomes as clear as the logic behind it.

You can easily find peace, joy and happiness in your tiny bubble within this world. And you can certainly find like

minded folks to fellowship with, share ideas and bond as friends.
And I hope you do.

But, the world is crazy.
There's violence and bad stuff everywhere. It's too easy to see.
And what you thought you knew about how the world works will change. I can promise that.

So before you bring another soul into this world, remember that it will not be the same for that person as it was for you. You didn't ask to be born into this. What do you think the next person will have to deal with?
I'm just asking.

Children (Chapter 6)

Please
For the love of all that is good and holy, think long and hard about bringing children into this world and what kind of world it will become for them.

Again, this is NOT a parenting book. Again, I did not attend an elite childhood development program at any ivy league school.
HOWEVER - I am a son and a father. And I'm deliberately observant.
So, I've learned a few things.

It's been said that none of us chose to be here. Basically, two people looked at each other, thought the other was cute and next thing ya know, here I am. We're almost all the result of uncontrolled hormones and bad decisions.

Should you procreate, know these things and know them well:

Children are designed and naturally geared to learn. They have NOTHING else to do.

They have no experience.
1. no understanding of limits
2. no understanding of norms
3. no regard for limits
4. do not recognize authority – authority does not compute – not a word yet

They have every reason to get what they want AND they have all the time in the world. They want (in no particular order):
1. your time
2. attention
3. things
4. food & drink
5. entertainment
6. things to learn

You will be forced to learn how they learn in order to teach them.
You will want to believe that you are the adult in charge. HAHAHAHAAAAAAA! Good luck.
You will discover that they can wear you down. They don't have jobs that suck the life out of them.
You do.
They have no bills or responsibilities or deadlines or any

drama.
You do.

WARNING: They can and will learn anything and everything.
Good or bad – doesn't matter. This is especially true of things you would rather that they don't learn.

Case in point: When my son was around 2 ½ years old, we were having lunch at a small, family restaurant that catered to the conservative farming community in a bible belt area. My father in law dropped his fork and muttered the F-word. Immediately, my sweet, innocent child's eyes lit up and he repeated the word PERFECTLY. He could barely say his own name, but as we tried to get him to NOT say the word, he giggled more and more and kept saying it louder and louder. Our faces were burning bright with humiliation as the entire building was howling in laughter at the toddler jumping up and down on the bench seat of our booth chanting at the top of his lungs, "FUCK! FUCK! FUCK! FUCK!"

Math, multiple languages, things you didn't learn until you were 20...
This is why "baby talk" should be avoided. Speak to them. They will learn. That's how they learn.
And don't be afraid to teach them anything in a logical order.

The evil side of children: Once they figure out how to manipulate you into giving them what they want... No matter the reason – to shut them up, get a moment of peace, or just too tired to parent - they will perfect that maneuver. They will pick, scream, cry, threaten, throw things and whatever else it takes to get what they want.

No one tells you how exhausted you will be for the first 5 years of each child's life. Because that's how long you have to stand your ground and be the "big meanie" in order to teach each kid to be a decent human and not abuse you into giving them everything they want when they want it.
Why should you make that 5 year battle?
Because if you don't, they will own you.
You will be their personal servant.
And they will be an insufferable, spoiled rotten hole of a human no one can stand.

Not teaching your children discipline – especially self discipline – is a complete injustice. They need that from you. They need you to teach them discipline.

Discipline is not punishment.
Punishment is a tool that helps teach discipline.
As with any tool, if it is over used, it will no longer be effective or useful. Use it wisely. You MUST use it, but you must use it strategically.

PLEASE* Whether you agree with me or not, please continue reading. I acknowledge that I will not change your mind or alter your beliefs. You can believe that I'm wrong on this topic.
But, please don't dismiss the experience and observations remaining in this book because you don't like this one section. It may not be for you, but I assure you that someone needs to hear this.

No physical punishment:

If you have allowed your relationship with your child to devolve to a point where the only time they do what you say is when you scream or threaten them, you have not instilled any discipline. The screaming and threats will have no real value because the kids know there is no REAL punishment. It's not reasonable to try to reason with a human that has not learned how to reason. Maybe it's possible to raise a decent human being without ever once spanking them. IF it is, I can't imagine the amount of intensity it must require to be vigilant every minute of every day. While I advocate that spanking should be rare and only used as a means of signaling a need to learn something immediately for safety or for lessons of paramount significance in life, never spanking is robbing your child of an important life lesson. Children NEED to learn that some things in life have severe consequences. I have seen families where the parents never used any physical punishments and the family situation spiraled into chaos. The first time physical "punishment" occurred was really just a gut level reaction of slapping their face when the child had gotten old enough and eloquent enough to use words so spiteful, hateful and painful that most likely any one receiving those words would have lashed out.

Excessive physical punishment:
If your child believes that you spank them for everything, they will believe it is impossible to do anything right in your eyes. Parents who over use physical punishment (basically beating their kids) are taking away the effectiveness of this tool. This includes the threat of physical punishment. It cannot be the only tool you have and employ.

Once kids figure out that the punishment is the same severity for any and all infractions, they no longer recognize any boundaries and begin to disregard your authority. The choices they make will only matter to them. They will not consider anyone else when making decisions and they will not care what consequences may be attached. After all, the spanking was used for everything. So, they may as well do what they want and take their whoopings.

Punishment must be moderate. Whether it's physical or any other format such as "time out." It is only a single tool in the tool box needed to achieve discipline. Discipline is learning a code of conduct and higher knowledge.
It's doing what needs to be done when it needs to be done.
It's doing what needs done regardless of how you feel. It doesn't matter if it's hard or easy. It doesn't matter about the weather, the time, the others around you or any other condition.
Know what is right and do it.
That's discipline.

Prepare for Parenthood (Chapter 7)

Preparing for Parenthood begins at birth.
Not the birth of your child. YOUR birth

My parents were teaching me how to be a parent by being a parent.

Of course they never thought of it that way. But, think about that now.

My parents were my first role models.

My sisters played with dolls. I did, too, but mine were army men and robots. We used those toys to imagine and act out feelings and emotions that we had, including feelings and emotions about our parents or what we thought a parent should be. It may have been indirect, but toys helped us explore thoughts and make fun of our parents and their rules or do things with our dolls that we thought our parents should do. Sometimes, it was just a way for us to exaggerate our interactions with our parents. Sometimes, we were just goofy kids making up a bunch of nonsense.

Other parents helped teach us about being a parent. When I went to the homes of friends, I saw how their parents treated them. I heard their interactions and watched how they got along together. I vividly recall one particular family I went to visit in Maryland. When I said I wished I had a family like theirs, they looked at me funny and asked why everyone said that same thing. I don't think they understood how rare they were.

School and teachers helped form ideas and thoughts to some extent. In my day, we had Home Economics where some kids took home dolls that were infant simulators. They cried and wet and needed fed. The class taught cooking, cleaning, home budget and other ordinary life skills for running a household. It was easy to mistake a teacher's professional persona for what we might image them to be as a parent if we thought of them as a good teacher. It has never really been uncommon for kids to confide in teachers and ask for advice.

Youth leaders were a major influence for some. After school programs, churches, or whatever field they might have come from gave some folks access to adults on a level that they might not have been able to experience at home. There's as many reasons why these relationships exist as there are people. Perhaps there was a missing parent. Maybe there was a gap in what was available at home for whatever reason. Not everyone had these kinds of people such as Big Brother/Big Sister volunteers. Some might have had CPS volunteers. But, some people were able to have relationships with adults that paralleled the relationships they had or should have had with their parents. While many were probably very good, some were definitely not. Despite any good intentions, people are people and people are not perfect. They have problems.

We simply do not live in a vacuum. We don't wear bubble wrap.
When we interact with people – kids or adults – we take in information, process that and form opinions and ideas. Some is intentional while some is very incidental. As we were growing up, we were absorbing information and using it to, well.... grow up!

That was the wildest and most unpredictable part of growing up – the people you would meet.
If you met good people with solid hearts and minds, you had access to good stuff.
If you were trapped in a hole with shitty people full of dead ideas and crud... well, you see where that leads.

Family (Chapter 8)

Blood is thicker than water.

Cute quote. Also BS. This is a very raw and maybe, brutal chapter of this book.

Look, we watched TV families. We watched. And the reason we watched was mostly because they were nothing like our family. It was pure fantasy escape.

Before I pull the pin on this, please take this seriously – there are good families. There are families out there that really care and love each other and get along and have fun family reunions. There are real families that really do get it and do it right. They have awesome lives. Of course they have problems. But, I'm talking about the ones that would NEVER end up on a talk show.

I would wager that great families are actually the minority.
Most families, I believe are a mix. They have the family members that are good as gold and usually, the matriarch of the family tree is the one that's pure gold. She's the one that holds the entire band together. She's why there's fun holidays and reunions. And sadly, when she's gone, there's no one else like her, and much of that unity dissipates.

These families also have a few bad apples.

You might even say, they have some rotten ones.
I'm not talking black sheep. I mean rotten. They exist.
Which means they have to exist somewhere, and it
could be in your family.

Some of these families will have cousins that are closer
than brothers and sisters. They may be best of friends
and hang around together as they grow up. They go to
school together and become the reason this cliché
exists. Blood is thicker than water. True here.

But
You know it. I know it. We all know it.
It's the worst and most brutal truth. Some people
should not reproduce. And it seems like the ones that
should not are able to pop out a kid every 9 months
while those that desperately want nothing more than to
have ONE kid and be the best parents they can possibly
be are not able to have any.

According to IndianaPrevention.org, 30%-40% of abuse
on kids comes from close family members. That's pretty
hard to ignore. They figure that 90% of abuse comes
from people the kids are close to, trust and love. Sounds
like "Stranger Danger" was a lie. It doesn't sound like
strangers are the real danger.

I'm not going to elaborate and tell horror stories. We all
know about it.
Family can be a drain on time, money, patience and
resources. They can lie and manipulate. There are
people that ruin their child's credit before the kid is out
of diapers. Look that one up.
Because of the closeness of family, manipulation is easy.

Stockholm syndrome is not just for kidnap victims. Point blank: biological relation is NOT an automatic obligation to remain close or faithful to "family." It does not guarantee anything good. It is NOT a contract and could actually be incredibly detrimental.

Blood can be more deadly than water.
(Ever hear of blood borne pathogens? They can be quite toxic and deadly. Just sayin.)

If you begin a family of your own, the family you knew growing up will be a blue print. It will either be a blue print you wish to follow, or it will be a reminder of all you want to avoid and NOT become, therefore it would be a blue print for escaping "the prison." It could most likely become a guidebook where you pick and choose which parts of being a parent you think your parents got right and which parts you think could have been done differently or better. It may become the blue print you adjust on the fly.

Ultimately, your family will be your responsibility. And there's a ridiculous amount of moving parts and variables in how that starts, forms, grows and exists. Prepare yourself.

Compatibility (Chapter 9)

Yes, I'm referring to finding a life long partner in crime.

Most people would make this a long, detailed chapter.
Nope.
It's not that hard.
It's not complicated.

It's a simple quiz.

1. Similar Taste – literally
2. Similar Taste – music and stuff
3. Same type and level of kink
4. Like minded

Similar Taste: Food.
Are you both spicy or mild? Do you both like the same foods prepared the same way? While a variance or two is fine, if there's a large gap between what you will share at meals EVERY DAY FOREVER, it's going to become an issue.

Similar Taste: Music, Movies, Entertainment, Activities.
Obviously, if y'all don't like a couple songs or films that the other does, it's not the end of the world. But if you have drastic differences in taste for music and movies, you'll end up spending a lot of time apart. This applies to forms of entertainment. If one likes festivals, the other needs to be equally as excited. The same goes for activities. If one likes to fish, the other should, too. Yes. You can have separate hobbies and interest and you actually should. The problem is when there are too many differences. A little time "in your own world" is good. At some point, you'll find that you're spending most of your time apart in your own worlds and bad things start to come of that.

Same type and level of kink: Yes. Sex stuff.
This is actually a major problem that drives couples to counseling. So, deal with it ahead of time. It's a deal breaker. And that's based on experience. Not just mine,

but many, many couples before you.
If one is into bondage, and other is not, it WILL be a major problem. No need to get graphic here. Just take this to heart. You NEED to be on the same wave length for sure.

That might mean you need to read and learn more, but don't commit with someone you can't keep up with or won't be satisfied with.

Like Minded: World Views.
This takes in politics, religion, education and every loose end you can think of. It's pretty simple. If there's a wide gap between y'all on any topic, it can lead to problems and arguments.
And that includes family.
When you marry (or move in) you get whatever is in the family as part of the package deal. You will be able to live YOUR life without the extended family MOST of the time. Sometimes, things happen and you have to live with someone's family for awhile.

Sometimes, a partner is much closer to their family than the other partner is with their family, resulting in more time being spent with one family and not the other. It doesn't sound like a big deal... until it becomes a big deal.

Factor in sports, hobbies, drinking/smoking habits, and how money is used in a relationship. If you don't address each of these items, they can become obstacles. And the only way to learn all this stuff is over time with deliberate intentions and honest conversations.

Some people "just know" and get married after 2 or 3 months. I have no numbers on success rates. Some people date for decades. That could be considered ridiculous by some folks, but if they ran the numbers and decided that marriage was not right, then marriage was not right. They're fine.

"Finding" someone that you want to spend the rest of you life with (or at least the majority of your life) is not something to be taken lightly. Once you bond, it's pretty savage to separate. I'd refer you to one of the many couples you no doubt have witnessed first hand to have fallen "so deep" in love then went completely soap opera when things fell apart.

I strongly suggest, in the most convicted way possible, that you consider compatibility to be paramount when dating and/or looking for a life long partner to "settle down with."
The last thing anyone wants is to be trapped in a loveless or hostile relationship.

Friends and Such (Chapter 10)

Get some.
Not party pals. Friends.
Someone that holds your hair for you to puke in the toilet COULD be your friend. But, if they talked you into getting that shit faced, no. No they are not.

A friend will help you become better than you are. The ones that hold you accountable to ideals, hopes and dreams are friends. They don't let you become a shitty person. They don't encourage you to become an alcoholic.

Your friends will be determined in part by common interest. Guys who want to play baseball tend to have friends that play baseball. Girls that love to create music tend to have musically inclined friends.
The single biggest determining factor in who you will become friends with is geography.

Hear me out. This is experience based and I'm speaking in general for my generation.
We tried having pen pals. (look it up)
We tried having ambassador exchanges.
We've tried long distance relationships of all sorts.
Yes, the internet changes that to some extent.
But, where you live determines who you have available to you.
My son had a hard time making friends at school.
Soon as we moved and he was in another school, he had no problem at all. (Yes, that's one small personal illustration – not a guiding principle to base everything on. But, you can see it helps make the point, right?)
No matter how much time you spend chatting online, it's not the same as being face to face. It can't replace touch and looking them in the eyes. In order to develop real friendships, y'all need to be in the same area.

The next biggest factor in who your friends will be when growing up is money. Not yours. Your parents.
That's because it matters what each of you can

contribute.

No one wants to carry the mooch. No one wants to always pay for everything for everyone.

And the kid that has a ton of money doesn't want to be liked because he has money. And he sure doesn't want the expectation that he will pay for everything for everyone just because he can. No one wants the feeling that they would be worthless to others if they don't fork out the money.

The smart one doesn't want his/her value tied to whether or not they do everyone else's homework. The brave one doesn't want to be the only fighter. Everyone has strengths and weaknesses. They don't want those traits to be their identity. We use terms like the rich kid, the poor kid, the smart kid, the big kid, the whatever-fits-before-kid kid. We describe each other by the most prominent trait. But, none of us want to be known just for that trait. And we certainly don't want to be liked or valued according to that trait.

It doesn't matter if it's right or fair. Your parents' economic status will play a huge part in who you have as friends. Rich kids will go on ski trips while poor kids shoot hoops at the public park. It really is that simple. And no movie or dream park can change that no matter how they write the script and who they pay to play the parts. That's life. That's real.

Now, you can be mad about that.
You can scream about inequality.
But, you can't change it.
That's how life works. What you CAN do is make the most of what you have. I'm not necessarily saying pretend that sticks and stones are play things and you

can create entire worlds and cultures with cardboard boxes and tape. Ya could. But... that's a rabbit trail.

Worry about your world. Do not compare.
Jealousy is the thief of joy. Comparison is the way to jealousy.
It doesn't matter what Jonny has. That's <u>his</u> world. What he has does NOT have any bearing on what you have. That stuff he owns is all HIS problem. Not yours. Just because he has certain things does not mean anything in your world. Think: how does Jonny's car alter your day? How does it affect you and what you have? What does it take from you? It takes nothing. It's just out there. You don't pay for it. You don't have to take care of it. That car does nothing for you. So, why waste time and energy and emotion on it?

Worry about your world.
How can you make the most of your time and money?
How can you improve your relationships and enrich your soul?
Where can you find the learning and resources you desire and crave that will allow you to become the person you long to be?
Learn to be disciplined.
Learn to do what needs to be done when it needs done.
Become the kind of person that money wants to find.
Become the leader people want in the lead.
Develop skills that put you in positions of power where you can make the decisions that change the bad things around you.
Go after the life you want where Jonny's car means nothing to you because you have everything and everyone you ever wanted and needed.

Yes, there's stuff in the way.
Clear that path. Go over it. Go around, through or under it. Blow it up or burn it down. Clearly, it's not going to be easy. So, what? If there's a pot hole in the road, do you get out of the car and give up going somewhere? Rhetorical question.

Like wise, if you're on a hike and there's a tree across the path, you don't turn back. You figure it out.
That's the magic sauce to success.
That's how filthy rich people became filthy rich. They figured it out.

And when you figure it out, you'll have the best of friends who probably helped you get there. And your kids will have the kind of friends they can brag to you about when they come home from skiing.

Some friends are only meant for a season.

So, you might make a new friend at something like a convention or youth conference or college. You know it's not forever. Before you even meet that person, you already know it's a limited engagement. The youth conference is only for a weekend or a week. Do you hold back? Probably not. (Yes, some will not make friends because they're afraid of the pain at separation because they're already played it all out in their head. Different story.)
You meet someone. Some goofy thing happens. Great conversations happen. You share a lot of personal stuff and bond. You know when you go your separate ways, the fabric of friendship will be torn. You tell each other

that you'll stay in touch, you'll never forget and this new friendship will never end.
But, it does.

That's ok.
Never hold back.
Never cheat yourself or anyone else out of the moment that could be one of the best moments in all of time. Live it. Embrace it. Feel everything clear to your socks. And when it's time to let go, don't let go easy. Don't cut the rope. Don't push them away. Let it hurt. Let is suck. Let the tears run down your face while you sob on the street or at the terminal.

Avoiding heartache and pain robs you of the opportunity to love deeply and feel real joy. Avoiding the pain robs you of the good. You can't avoid the bad without missing out on the best. Go home and cry for 3 days. Stop eating and just cry for 3 days. And when you come out on the other side, you'll have memories that don't just echo in your head, but ring true in your heart.

There's nothing else to say here.

Actually, I lied.
There is one more thought needed here.

Friendships (P.S. or coda or afterthought or whatever)

We start developing friends from the earliest of ages. It's not magic. It's not fate.
It's simple human nature and time.
Remember, kids are designed and wired to learn. That includes friendship.

Preschool and birthday parties, time with cousins and play dates with kids in the neighborhood: these opportunities allow young ones to learn what friends are and are not.

As kids grown up, they spend time playing, fighting, laughing, crying, arguing and learning first hand all the emotions that will surround them the rest of their lives. With some role modeling and input from parents, kids can learn social norms and figure out how to control feelings and make the most of them.

But the bonds that form over time while riding bikes and playing games or sports will last. Or maybe those bonds will break. It's a little bit of a crap shoot. There will probably be times when friends fight and split then make up and re-bond. Few relationships are smooth all the time. And since kids are learning as they go, it's not likely that relationships will be smooth all the time. Hard times, fun times and sad times will become memories forever.

For most of us, we will remember many of the kids we grew up with all our lives. We'll still remember many of our classmates from elementary school and high school. We will remember several college mates. From there, we may forget most of the people we meet that do not stay in our life for extended periods like say a work environment. Obviously, those that move around as kids will have a very different experience.

But, by college age, most of us have found that one friend that we call our best friend. We may have a small circle of friends that we cherish and adore, but there'll be **one** best friend.

Military (and front line responders) will most likely have their Band of Brothers that they're bonded to for eternity. Those relationships will be unique. And they'll be strong.

The overwhelming truth is that the universe did not bring the perfect person to us. Life happened and we bonded with the people available to us. Our friendships and our best friend just happened to be someone we clicked with and forged those bonds. If we feel "perfection" like we found the perfect person, then that's what it became, because we made that happen. We didn't plan it. We didn't decide. But, we still made it happen.

It's ok to believe it's fate or providence.
But, psychologically speaking, we're designed to bond and build a community for ourselves... a support system of sorts. We don't need a specially designed person to bond with. We just need people.
We will filter them out.

Over time, goals and dreams, likes and hates, activities and hobbies will all help us filter through the humans available to us and we will find our best friend. It's not magic. It's just the way life works.

Maturity (Chapter 11)

We mature as we age. But only to a point.
We grow up. And we stop "growing up." Then, we just grow old.

There' a joke that says, "I don't know how to act my age, because I've never been this old before."

Let's spell out the obvious:
1. Everyone matures at a different rate
2. Everyone matures to a different degree (or level)
3. Not everyone actually matures or "grows up"
4. A few will mature to a point so far beyond the average that they come off as boring and arrogant because the rest of us can't relate to them.

Now that we have the petty arguments under control – and there's an understanding that the following is a generalization - I'd suggest that our mentality stops aging around the age of 25.

I used to photograph high school sports in my 30s and 40s.
I didn't feel that far removed in my mind from where those kids were in their minds. I could clearly remember (and even feel) much of the emotion of the cheer block and the thrill of sports and the confusion over the opposite sex, and how much homework sucked and the terror of realizing at 11pm that there was a test the next day I wasn't prepared for.

Now, obviously, I'm looking at it from the other side

with hindsight.
But, the simple truth here is that those kids were looking at me like I was a dinosaur! They thought I must have escaped from a museum somewhere.

And before the witch hunt begins, I am clearly stating that I never wanted to be "one of the guys" with a bunch of adolescent teens. That's not even a thing. Every time I talked to them, I felt like a high school kid at lunch with my 3rd grade sibling. Those who know me know I don't like kids at all. (And yes, I know. I've already been demonized for not liking kids. Whatever. Back to the point.)

When I say that our maturing or "growing up" stops at 25, it's not a hard and fast rule. It may be more like it mellows out or levels off. Those of us over 40 can honestly admit that we didn't change much in our thinking or feelings after 25-ish.

There's simply no substitute for experience. And by age 40, we've accumulated a lot of experience we did not have at 25. So, we process things differently. Or maybe we process stuff more effective and efficiently. It's really quite easy to see a situation developing and say to ourselves, "Oh, I've seen this before." In fact, we often use the expression, "Been there. Done that."

It's a bit of subtle nuance really.
We still get butterflies when we see someone that's amazingly attractive. But, we have learned what that really means and how to deal with it in a way that prevents us from looking like love sick puppies drooling on ourselves.

We still get excited to do well on something that tests our skills.
We just know how to celebrate it better.
We have better judgment on taking risks, because we've been beat up, broken and defeated a few times. We consider options and make serious calculations before attempting anything risky because we know that we need our jobs to pay our bills and we know our insurance will go up (or drop us) for taking unnecessary risks. It's that "old enough to know better" thing. We have simply been around long enough to not be able to claim ignorance. No one would believe us.
We tend to hide our emotions better because we've seen what others may do with them. We certainly have the emotions, but we've experienced real world trolls and demons. So, now we guard them.

I'm not trying to tell you NOT to have feelings or to hide them and suppress them. Not at all! Actually, you NEED to experience all of them and set them out on display and be bold in expressing them!
Why?
You're young.
It's understandable at your age. It's forgivable.
And it's fixable.

You're still growing, learning and developing.
You can fix things in you. You can right the wrongs.
You can learn from everything and use that information and experience for the rest of your life.

Image how hard it is to unlearn something.
You always set your drink to the right. You get a new desk/seat. The only place for you to set your drink is on

the left. Good luck not trying to set it off to the right! Or try learning to do something with your "other hand." That's why you need to learn young. Once you're older, it's hard. Trying to "fix yourself" after you've had 40 years of breaking... that's not a good spot to be.

There are many people who married young. They've only known a singular, monogamous relationship for a good part of their adult life. Suddenly, they're divorced or their spouse "ran off."
Now what?

On one hand, it's a "do over."
They get to redesign and rearrange their lives any way they want.
Most likely they will not.
Most likely they will do what they did before. It'll look different, but it won't be. And they'll wonder why they ended up with the same results.
Some will find the exit and start over and do well.
Most will start over about ¼ to ½ way along the same trail and do what they've always done.
Why do I say this?
Because I know how many people order the same thing at every restaurant.

You had a good thing going and it ended? That sucks.
Now it's time to grow up.
It's time to set aside all the things you thought you knew and all the ways you learned in your youth and learn new things. It's time to make new choices. It's time to set up new ways and habits and decisions and choices.

It's not time to do what you did. After all, it didn't work! If it feels comfortable or familiar or "right," there's a strong chance it's not good. Think about that. If you do something and say out loud, "Well, that didn't go as planned," then it's time to try something different!

It's easy to say, "They just weren't ready. They needed to grow up more. There was something wrong with them."
Maybe you're right. So, don't go with the same feelings, plans and measuring stick and expect different results. Because, that's how you got someone that was "messed up."

Here is where maturity and discipline come in handy. Just knowing what is right and what to do isn't enough. Making the hard, lonely decisions that hurt is what needs to happen. That's being mature.

Crying and looking for help worked as a kid. As an adult (grown up) it's kinda a pathetic. YES, you may need help. Don't get bogged down in semantics here. Be mature. IF you need help, get help. You understand the intention here.

Let's say bad and terrible things happen to you at 40. If you handle it the way someone at 18 would, you will be judged.
Those younger people will be conflicted, because they haven't been where you have been and they're looking to you for understanding the road ahead. If you can't do better than they can do, where does that leave them?

No one will fault you for crying. No one will blame you

for getting mad and throwing things... for a minute. But, once the smoke clears and initial punch in the gut settles, there's an unspoken expectation that you will "handle it like an adult." You'll be held accountable to be mature. People may not say anything. But, that reality will be present.

The problem here is that we are not taught how to be THAT mature!
There's no classes on that. There's counseling once the fall out begins, but there's no prep and no instruction manual. We end up reaching a "new level of mature" each time we clean up from tragedy.

Your pet dies. You learn.
You lose parents or friends. You learn.
You wreck a car. You learn.
And it sucks. It hurts. And it ruins a lot of stuff in you and your life.
Think of the term "innocence lost."
You catch your Significant Other cheating. You learn. Oh, my! How you really do learn a lot in a short amount of time.

The broken pieces hurt more than stepping barefoot on those plastic building blocks left on the floor. Each time this happens, you grow. You probably didn't want to, and you were definitely not ready. But, it happens. That's just how life rolls on us.

By the time we're 25, we've had enough pain and suffering to reach a solid level of maturity. After that point is crested, there's not much further to go. After all, once you reach the summit of a climb, you can't go much higher – just look around and take notes.

Once we've reached that level, I believe things level off or mellow out.
We're still the person we've become, but we know more.
We've experienced most of the crap (and good) life has to throw at us.... not all... but enough to develop a real sense of expectations.
From there, we have learned to formulate responses or coping mechanisms. We can't predict the future or prepare for EVERY possible scenario or situation, but we're as prepared as possible and fairly well equipped to face the world.

I can summarize maturity from peaking at 25 in this: When we were young and called "cute," we had a silly, childlike response. When we're mature, we don't like to be called "cute" so much, but rather beautiful (or handsome), and we have a more tempered response. And we understand what is being said and why.

Success & Money (Chapter 12)

Sometimes success is a matter of just showing up. Sometimes it's not giving up.

Figure out what people want and then figure out how to get them to pay you for it. This is the most simple of laws for the rich.

People say that money will always come back to you or

that you can make more money. This is not really true. You will need to find a balance between using money now and saving money for later in life. The one thing you can be sure of is that YOU will be the only one responsible for taking care of you both now and later. The problem is that "it takes money to make money" is not just a cleaver saying.

Let's back up from that a second.

Here's the perfect summary of needing money:
When you're 16, you need a car.
To get the car, you need a job.
To get the job, you need a car.
Now, that could be different in a city with public transportation, but outside of the major metros, that's the way life works.
It's not always possible to get what you need to get started without help.

Now apply this problem to life when you're on your own and maybe have a family to take care of. If you become unemployed with no income for any reason - just play along with this scenario and feel it -
The first check from starting a new jobs tends to be at least 2 weeks out. Food, shelter, power, gas for car, are critical things that require immediate money. In fact, to get the job, you must have transportation, clean clothes and appear kept and decent. If you find yourself homeless for any reason – how do you acquire these basic things necessary to get and keep a job? How can anyone pull themselves up by the boot straps when they have no boots?

What I'm saying here is that it is entirely possible to get

so far down in the hole, that it becomes impossible to get yourself out of the hole. The ONLY way out is with help. And it will take a LOT of help. And it will take a long time. How many people do you think are willing to give that much help for that long? How long would you be willing and able to help someone that ran out of money (and luck) and needed to start over completely? Considering that most people live paycheck to paycheck, I don't think very many could help that much. And I believe that the ones that might have the resources would be limited in patience on helping to such a great extent for so long.

Here's an over simplified money exam for illustration.

When my kids were born at the end of the 90s:

$10/hr x 40 hr/wk = $400
Tax will take about 25% leaving $300
$300 x 4 weeks = $1200/mo

That's income.

IF monthly living expenses are:
rent = $400
Gas = $100
Electric = $100
Water = $30
Sewer = $30
Trash = $20
Car payment =$200

That's $880/mo of basic living expenses.

$1200 in - $880 out = $320 for food, gas, entertainment and everything else.

Oh, wait.
Insurance could be $100/mo.
and I forgot money for license renewals.
And I didn't mention home internet or cable or TV or anything like that.

This is 2023.
Just double all numbers and you get the same results.
The picture here is that it takes a lot of money to just exist.
Imagine what it takes to get someone with nothing up to that speed WHILE doing this for yourself at the same time. How many people do you know that can support someone long enough to get them back "on their feet" to where they have this income and all that goes with it?

Now let's talk 401K.

My grand parents worked in coal mines and on the railroad.
They started out making .50¢/hr. I vaguely remember one of them talking about making .15¢/hr. They saved some of that for retirement.
By the time they retired, they were making almost $10/hr in whatever job they had. How much money do you think they were able to save at less than $2/hr? And how much do you think things would cost by the time they were making $10/hr?

Do you see how they were saving in their early years for

a world that would cost 8x more than what they were able to plan for?

When I was able to begin working at the age of 16, I was dreaming of how awesome it would be to make $10/hr. That seemed like a ridiculous amount of money. Last year, I was making $25/hr and could barely afford the basics of life in America. In fact, I didn't have home internet, because I couldn't afford it with one income in the house. I was only on the internet through my phone.

A retirement plan is supposed to allow you to stash money away all your working career so that when you get old enough to retire, there's money there for you. The plan is for your money to make more money as it "sits there." Truth is that someone is making money with your money and you're getting some of that. Or you will *eventually* get some of that.

But, as many have discovered, when the stock market drops, so does the money in your 401k.
You could lose thousands of dollars.
I'm not saying not to have one.
I'm just warning you that it's not exactly everything they tell you.
It's not 100% safe and certainly not a fool proof guarantee.

To be fair, the pandemic was an unusual event in the investing world called a Black Swan. No one could see it coming. It was not predicted.
And the market crashed.

But, investing – which is how a 401k makes money, is risky business, even in the best of times.

And honestly, there's no guarantees at all. People used to get a "good job" and expect to retire from the company with a pension. Pensions are now a thing of the past.
Many of the companies that paid them are gone.
Companies close and industries change.
Technology gets replaced.
Computers took the place of typewriters, so everyone in the typewriter industry lost their job.
It's currently believed that anyone entering the work place now, will have to change careers – not jobs...
CAREERS – as much as 7 times before retirement!

So, it would seem wise to always be looking ahead.
I'd suggest you keep learning about new technology and where the world is heading. Keep improving skills and learning new ones, so that when a job change is needed, you can make that transition.

Making Money (Chapter 13)

This is a fun one.

Actual conversation:
Characters – ME and the Hotel Owner from Pakistan (HOP)

HOP: What brings you to my hotel?

ME: I'm at the fairgrounds photographing horses all weekend.

HOP: What?

ME: I photograph horses.

HOP: And people pay you?

ME: Yes.

HOP: You take pictures of horses... animals that people ride.... and people pay you enough money that you can come stay in my hotel and eat at a restaurant?

Me: Yeah.

HOP (long pause as a huge smile blazes across his face and hands finally fly up in air): I LOVE THIS COUNTRY!! THIS IS THE GREATEST COUNTRY IN THE WORLD!! THERE ARE SO MANY WAYS TO MAKE MONEY!!"

He's not wrong.

Now before you go dreaming about starting a company and being a millionaire off of social media, let's clear up a couple dubious illusions.

1. Work/Life Balance – great buzz phrase that's an illusion. If you work a "real job," you will EITHER have time OR money – not both. You will spend your time making money, or you will have time because you're not making money. Fact. Big facts.

2. There is more money to be made in knowing things than doing things.

   A. The ones who do the "mindless" manual labor (even though there's no such thing as mindless) get paid the least.

   B. The ones that do the least actual work get paid the most because they know stuff. Such as engineers and executives.

3. You will NEVER get paid what you're worth. Just a simple fact.
4. There really are a LOT of ways to make a living/money/good life. ALL of them require knowledge. You're gonna have to learn a lot. And that's ok.

Hear me on this – If you don't learn anything else from this book, hear this right here:
In order to earn money, you will have to learn stuff.
There is NO other way.
So, learn how to learn.
Learn how to be educated and remember things.
Find out how much you don't know.
Figure it out. Figure out how to figure things out.

There is not one single job on this planet where you can get paid without knowing stuff. Even if you get paid to stand there and look good, you STILL have to figure out and know how to get paid for it.
YOU ARE GOING TO HAVE TO LEARN STUFF IF YOU WANT MONEY.

Do you know why the manager gets paid more than the person doing the work?
Do you really believe that they are more important?
Do you think they're really smarter?
It's not magic. And it's not intelligence.
They just know the things that are required for the position that owners and board members believe are worth paying for.
They learned the language.

They learned the behaviors and protocols.
They learned the math and book keeping and programs.
They went to college where they learned to get by and meet deadlines and follow the curriculum.
They learned to do what was expected of them over the course of several years.
They learned to avoid trouble and how to appear to be in good standing.
They learned how to navigate the corporate waters.

All they learned how to appear to be valuable to those with the money.
And above all, they learned to assign value to themselves so that they only agree to work for more money. It may not be what they are worth, but it's what they have been able to sell themselves for so far.
They learned to sell their knowledge and experience at top dollar.
They chose a path where money can be made by knowing things rather than using their body to move stuff around or weld or build or glue parts.

No matter what path you take, you will have to learn stuff.
You can learn simple stuff like working a broom.
Or you can learn complicated stuff like programming.
Or you can learn corporate language and everything that goes with it.

Learn to learn.
And learn to love learning.
This is the way.

Weather the Storm (Chapter 14)

Without storms, nothing grows.
It's going to rain. It's going to get rough. That's just part of the world we live in.
Sure, it would be nice to live in a perfect system where it's always sunny and pleasant and there's never any rough weather. But, that's rare or, most likely, not real.

Storms will come, both physical and metaphorically speaking.
All you can do is weather the storm.
Ignore all the "what ifs." ALL OF THEM.
Those are only important when PREPARING for storms.
"What if the wind?" "What if the rain?" "What if someone lies?" "What if I lose my job and someone dies or a flood comes or the car breaks down and... ?"

It's going to happen.
The cliché is that IF it can go wrong it will, and it will do so at the worst possible time.
Anyone who has ever been in the infantry will tell you to never ask if it can it get any worse because they already know that YES IT CAN!
It doesn't matter how bad it is, it can ALWAYS get worse.

You have to ask all those "what if" type questions when things are calm or good so you can prepare as much as possible in advance.
"What if money?" = Save and plan for financial hardships or large expense items.
"What if sick?" = Health insurance and a help network in case you get injured and need people.

"What if flood?" = Have a plan of escape and a place to go BEFORE the rains start.

There's an endless list of "what if."
You can't really have a solid plan for everything, because you can't possibly know every possible "what if." You can't know all the problems out there.
HEAR THIS AND EMBRACE IT: You can't worry about them all, either.

All you can do is all you can do.
"But, I don't like thinking about that stuff. It makes me anxious."
NO KIDDING!! No one likes to think about it, but how much worse will you feel when it happens and you're not prepared? This is why discipline is so important. Do what needs done when it needs done. In this case, BEFORE there's a need.
Plan. Save. Prepare. Learn things. Watch and pay attention.
We can learn from the past.
We know what tornadoes can do.
So, we plan for food and water in a safe shelter with emergency lighting and necessities to survive a couple days IF the worst case scenario becomes reality. Odds are that we will never actually be in a tornado, but the odds are never zero. And the illustration makes the point.

And when the storm comes, all you can do is hunker down and ride it out. Weather the Storm.
Someone dies or gets sick. You can't change it.
You can only weather the storm.
Your lover left you. You can't make them come back.

You can only weather the storm.
If you are alive, there will be storms. You will have to endure them and whatever they bring.
You will have to weather the storm, whether you like it or not.
So, do all you can to prepare yourself.

The worst part of storms is the aftermath.
Once the thunder rolls and the clouds clear and the rains stop, it's time assess the damage. Natural storms can down limbs and whole trees. Flood waters can be left behind. Buildings can be damaged or destroyed. Our personal storms can result in trust issues, damaged self esteem, lacking self confidence and a host of other issues.
The only thing that can be done is to survey the damage.
Take inventory and assess needs.
Then, get to work fixing things.

You can wait for rescue, and if you really need rescued, you should definitely do everything you can to get the attention you need. If you need help, call for help!
No one will think anything bad.
In fact, moments like that are the reason we have people trained to help.
Call on them.
Please.

Get help. Help others.
And be ready for everything to grow.
Because not only will the lawn grow because of the rain, so will mold on things that got wet and don't get dried out. Damage cost might grow. You see where this is

going.

So, weather the storm.
Get help if you need it.
Give help if you can.
Look around and get to work.
The next storm will be coming eventually.
Be ready.

Be True to You (Chapter 15)

We've all heard the cliché, "To thine own self be true" or "Be true to yourself." Catchy. Have you ever really thought about that?

People always have a reason or excuse for what they do. At least when they get older. But truth and right moral values are always true and right regardless of actions. And actions always result in consequences regardless of intentions.

Bad behavior is always bad.
Yeah, I know all the jokes about good times being made because of bad decisions. I'll even confess to being guilty of such things. I contend that there is a distinct difference between "bad decisions" like jumping your bicycle over a picnic table and truly bad behavior that is actually bad character or lack of decency. People can be rude, crude and down right disrespectful. That's bad behavior.

While it can be easy to sympathize with people, and often, we want to give people the benefit of the doubt, you need to remain true to yourself. You may know them. And you truly want to help for all the right reasons.

However -

The need to cling to YOUR values, morals, safety and sanity is critical.

People will use you. It may or may not be intentional. They may not even realize that they do it. People will lie to you. People will take as much as you are willing to give. Then, they'll ask for more. The more you give, the more they take. People will use you up till you're depleted and broken. Then they'll ask you what's wrong.

You can end up giving yourself away.

If you don't set limits, you end up drained. Without limits and boundaries, you will become empty and resentful. Once you've become empty and drained, you will find it nearly impossible to refill yourself. And you'll find it hard to find anyone willing to give to you the way you gave to others.

This is not to say that we should never help others and never share our time and talents and resources.

It IS a warning to do so with clear limits and boundaries.

It's a plea to set expectations BEFORE giving all you have.

Because a hard truth is that "takers" have no boundaries.

By all means, giving of yourself and helping others is

good, right, noble and worthy. I'd suggest it's even necessary to become a better version of you.

I'm also suggesting, that it's best to keep in mind that you're not Superman or Batman or any other super hero. You're a finite human with limited resources, both external and internal.
Never lose sight of that.

The Truth is Always True (Chapter 16)

I guess the title really says it all.

But, I say that because people lie.
Everyone single person. They/We all lie.
Some do it to avoid hurting your feelings.
Some will lie to make you feel better about something.
Some tell "white lies" to avoid bad things.

Many lie to avoid consequences of their actions.
They lie to police about how fast they were driving or what they were doing.
They lie to parents to avoid punishment.
They lie to teachers to avoid bad grades or detention or suspension.

Some will lie to get what they want.
They tell you they love you so they can use you.
They tell you things that make you trust them so they can take advantage of you.
They lie to you to take your money or possessions.

You can't change it. You can't fix it.
People are people and people are dumb.
And people lie. That's just one of the major flaws in people.
That's the way they are and will always be no matter how much wishing we do.

But the truth will always be true.
It doesn't matter how anyone "spins" it.
It doesn't matter how they twist it.
It doesn't matter if they lie or how much they lie.
The truth will always be true.
Period.

An important thing to understand and embrace is that nothing changes the truth AND people will lie. This means that someone will do something wrong or illegal or immoral, then lie to cover it up. One of the most common tactics used to throw you off the trail or to avoid consequences is when they try to make you prove anything and everything.

While the legal system is justly built on the premise of "innocent until proven guilty," this is NOT true in most personal issues. Trying to prove guilt does not change the truth. You may not be able to prove they said something, but you know. You may not be able to catch them cheating red handed, but you know.
You both know.

Sometimes knowing the truth is enough.
No proof necessary.

Despite all their efforts to cover the lie, they can not cover the truth.

The other most common tactic people use to throw you off of their trail when they lie or cheat or do something wrong, immoral or illegal is to accuse YOU of the very thing that <u>they</u> are guilty of. If they can get others questioning you, and get you on your heals trying to prove that you are innocent, they believe that no one will investigate them. Accusing you of the crime they committed gives them a place to hide in plain sight.

While you are running around ducking arrows, they're sitting back laughing. They cheat on you, then accuse you of cheating. Now your head is spinning as you frantically try everything in the world to prove you're not cheating. Meanwhile, they're still cheating and smugly enjoying the show as they watch your head spin. They know you know. They know that you know that they are cheating. But you can't prove it and you're defending yourself. You have no time or energy to prove that they are cheating. They feel like they're winning.

But the truth is still true.
They're cheating. You are not.
NOTHING can change that.

Taking definitive action in this type of circumstance is not easy. You know what is right. You know what is true. But feelings mess with your head. The feelings of being judged and feeling like you have to prove something before taking action can be paralyzing. But, nothing changes the truth. Feeling helpless and hurt and all the doubts and sickening feelings is overwhelming.

But, the truth will set you free.

You may not want to be set free. You may not like it.
But, being bound to a lie and a liar is punishment. Let
the truth set you free.
Let it set you free from guilt.
It will set your mind free from doubt.
Turn your heart over to the truth and let it live free.

The truth is always true.
And you should be, too.

My Words to the Youngest (Chapter 17)

If you are the first born, that's ok. Do NOT skip this
chapter.

Dear Second Child – and All Younger Siblings:

We didn't know.
When we had your older sibling, we didn't know.
It's really that simple.
We were ignorant of all we had gotten into.
We had NO idea how much we didn't know.
We were unprepared regardless of how much we tried
to prepare.
We were kids learning as we went.
We didn't know how much we didn't know.

All the things you didn't get to do or were not allowed
to do because of your older sibling is because we

learned the hard way with them and only wanted everything to be better for you.

It's not your fault.
Whether you were planned or not.
There's nothing wrong with you.
You could NOT have possibly understood why things were the way they were.

But we did.
We just didn't know to communicate that to you.
And even if we thought we could, you were simply not prepared to process that information.
We were kids learning how to raise kids.

If you ever accused your parents of having a favorite child, you're probably not wrong, but still owe them an apology. Sound ridiculous? Of course. So was your accusation. It was manipulative. It was intended to hurt and it was unfair and you know it.

"We love you all the same." = lie.
Not possible. At least that's how it feels on the surface. You may all come from the same gene pool, but none of you are the same. I had 2 kids and could not have planned 2 more different humans. You and your siblings are NOT the same. So, it's not possible to love you all the same. You're unique. Your relationship with your parents is unique. Your understanding of your place in the world, the family and the universe is unique.

Your parents are not the same people at your birth as they were at the birth of each sibling. Yeah, yeah, they are, but no they're not. You know what I mean about learning and growing as they went.

The truth is that your parents would have tried to show you equal love and love you as much as you think they loved the others.
They loved you each uniquely; a unique love and relationship with each child. They would have a unique love for you.
And that was designed especially just for you.

That is to say that "Love you all the same" really means that they love you as much as the other in a unique way.

That being said:
If you had good parents, it was because they had done all they could to be good people. If you had shitty parents, odds are they were shitty people. It's really that simple.
Yes, everyone makes mistakes.
But, let's be honest – methheads are just not likely to be great parents. Maybe. But the odds are obviously not in favor. Abusive people, narcissist, rapists, pedophiles, drug dealers, alcoholics, and other such categories are... shall we say... problematic and not likely to make great role models. And parents are by default role models.

Let's be even more honest – just because someone goes to church and pays their taxes, does NOT automatically make them a great role model. Many "upstanding citizens" have been monsters hiding in plain sight. People can appear to be "good people" while hiding a ridiculous list of bad traits that have been taken to extremes such as controlling, manipulative, obsessive, jealous, *ad infinitum*.

The making of a decent human is rather difficult to define. There's too many parameters and variables. It's a balance. Actually, it is not A balance... it IS balance. Actually, it's the most impossible balancing act in existence. Firm- fair- open- decisive- protective- fostering- governing- giving- permitting- preventing, etc etc.

It's an endless, exhaustive balance between extremes all at once.

Yet, oddly, it's attainable and actually expected.

A good parent is the result of being a decent person and learning how the world works and what makes for good people and success and fulfillment.

Let's make it simple.

Can a shitty person teach someone to be a good person?

If "lead by example" matters, no.

It's really that simple.

Now the trouble with life and the world is universal understanding and agreement on what makes a decent person. There's not a set standard for good or decent. In times of dictatorships, yes – standards were not only clear, but enforced. Examples: Salem witch trials, Nazi Germany, the Dark Ages.

There are very clear expectations and guidelines in strict cultures or societies, such as Amish, Russia, and most middle eastern countries.

We're in America, the Melting Pot. Land of the Free. It's easy to believe that the 10 commandments are the single most fundamental moral compass. After all, "Not Murder" seems pretty sane and logical. Plus, the rest of the Bible can be very instrumental in providing "herd direction." I know that sounds like a ridiculous way to put it, but when there's one book of guiding values, it really does provide a uniform set of expectations and behavior. It's like a code of conduct. It's like a map to good morals and character. (Yes, for those that have been to seminary, I know that's not what the Bible is there for and I know the Roman Road... yes, yes... This book is not intended for theological doctrine. Roll with me here. Please. Ya can't argue that the good book makes a solid case for being a decent person.)

In another moment of brutal honesty: the Bible really narrows the path (pun intended) and this allows bad people to use it to control others. Yes, I'm admitting that the good book has been used for bad intentions like control and manipulation. This goes with the truth that "No system is any better than the people in it." Sorry. That includes, the church and religion. Before you argue – reread those words.
Good people = good
Bad people = bad
This goes for the church and religion, too.
Plain and simple and honest. Period.
It has NOTHING to do with what is true. Nothing can alter the truth. And the truth is that good and bad both exist.
And they exist everywhere. So choose good.
The bad people do not nullify the truth that the Bible provides.
(So, yeah, ya got me. I really do believe the Bible is true. If you don't, I understand. No need to fight me on this. I will only stand by

the truth that the truth is always true no matter what.)

This leads me to the matter of honesty.

Everyone is EITHER:
Trying to let you know that you can trust them
or
Trying to make you FEEL LIKE you can trust them.

These are very different people.

An honest person wants to be known as honest. They value honesty and want others to know that they are trustworthy because of being honest.

A dishonest person also wants to be known as honest. That's the only way they can be dishonest. After all, they are not trustworthy.
Therefore, they need to be seen as honest so they can hide the truth.

Honest folks just do what is right.
Dishonest people lie and then lie to cover the lie. They steal and act like it wasn't them. They do things that are deceitful and become deceitful. Their entire existence becomes a fraud. Their face is a facade and their name is a front. They're fake.

So, how do you tell the difference?
Well, sometimes you can't.
Liars can become so good at lying that they believe their own lies.
It becomes part of them. It becomes the only way they know. Many times, you can feel dishonesty. You may not

be able to prove anything, but you know. Proving and knowing are 2 very different things.

Don't waste your time trying to catch them or prove anything.
They will keep you chasing your tail trying to catch them in a lie. They intentionally smear your nose in the "fact" that you can't prove that they are deceitful. They are entertained by you as they watch you go nuts trying to prove it. They'll even see how far they can stretch the truth just see how far you'll chase your tail.
Do not waste time or energy on this.

Once you've identified the problem, eliminate it from your life as soon as possible. This is the ONLY solution. You can't fix them. You can't win. You can't make it better in any way. Sorry. That's how this works.

They have to WANT to be honest AND take aggressive action towards shedding dishonesty and becoming an honest person in all ways.

Buy a House (Chapter 17)

This is the most necessary trap you will ever buy into.

If you live in a major metro area, this may not be a real option. Do what ya gotta do. You might be better off anyway. Renting always allows an option to leave more easily.

THE HOUSE RULES

You may pay for the house and say you own it, BUT...
Whatever you own will own you.
You will become a slave to all that own.

So, do NOT buy the biggest, most elaborate house you can. Especially if it's your first house.

1. The Loan – This is generally the most significant expense in everyone's income. Simply look up a loan calculator and put in some numbers. Watch how much you end up paying over 30 years. Yeah... no joke 2X or 3X the original cost. AND if you ever default, they can and will come take your house away to pay your outstanding debt, even if it's only $1,000.

2. Repair/Replace – appliances and furniture wear out. Everything you have will eventually be old and worn and ugly and outdated. (Look up Harvest Gold from the 70s) As much money as you will be shelling out on the mortgage, you will need more for furniture, a new stove, a new washer and/or dryer, water pump, water conditioner, furnace or whatever.

3. The Building and Grounds: paint, siding, windows, roof, grass, lawn care, driveway, garage, gutters, and a myriad of small things like filters for furnace and water filters will eat up various chunks of money over time.

4. Insurance – greatest organized crime in the world right behind government. But, ya gotta have it.

5. Taxes – Oh... speaking of government

6. Operating expenses: gas, water, electric, trash,

internet, entertainment, food, etc.

You'll worry about it while on vacation. You'll be mad that you're always at work and barely get to enjoy the place, because when you're not at work, you're working on the house. You'll be frustrated that you want to go have fun, but have to mow the lawn.

The kids will destroy it. Not all at once, but over time - crayons, drinks, food, holes, burns, and things you can't imagine will happen. Speaking of destroy, if you want pets, take lots of "before pictures" when you move in. LOL Sucker! You gonna learn.

Now obviously, if you make truck loads of money, you can hire people to do things for you. However, if you're young and starting out, one of the best terrible experiences you can have (that's no mistake on what I said) is to buy the worst house on a good street.
Get it at a great price because it's rough.
Gut it and fix it up. Make it the best place on the street while living there. Then, sell it for more than you have in it.
Do this twice. You'll learn so much, it's insane. You'll appreciate what you have 100X more than your friends ever will appreciate what they have. And if you do it right and spend wisely, you might not have much of a house payment on your third home which could become your forever home.

Now to be fair, you NEED a decent house, especially as you approach your 30s and seriously as you near 40. Your home is your castle. There's a reason this gets said.

It's where you raise your kids and teach them to be decent humans.

It's where you decompress after work.

It's where you relax when time allows.

There's pride in a decent home that's kept up... or better yet, one you fixed up to be great!

It's where you keep your possessions and memories.

You host holidays and birthdays there. You might plant a garden or raise flowers.

Everything you do and everything about you revolves around your house. That's your home base. You're safe. You rest.

You live, love, fight, dream, argue, struggle, succeed and win within these walls.

It's were you'd rather poop more than any other place on earth.

When you're having a bad day at work, you'll hardly be able to wait to get home.

You'll be relieved to be home after an exhausting but wonderful vacation. There will be times it will drive you crazy, but there'll be times when you can't explain how wonderful it is to own a home. You'll lose sleep over it and invent new swear words because of it.

But, it will always be home.

A final thought on buying a house when you're young - Your junior year of high school, get a part time job. Save all you can. Spend some. You're young. Enjoy and live a little. Just a little. But save all you can. Work that job for 2 years while living with your parents rent free and eating their food. (Obviously, if you have shitty parents, this doesn't work. I'm sorry.) Once you graduate, get a full time job. SAVE EVERYTHING YOU CAN. Yes, you'll have to spend some, but save all you can while living at home.

Do not rent an apartment! Do not buy dumb stuff! Save money.
After 4 years of saving, you might have enough for a decent down payment on your first house.

Now I know that when we hit 18, we can't wait to be free and live life on our own terms and get away from Mom and Dad's rules. And if you go to college, that's a different path.
But do not get an apartment just to "be free."
Suck it up and live at home. Get a house.
You'll be 10 years ahead of your peers with that 4 years of work.

And if you think you're going to get an apartment with your buddies or friends... DO NOT. There's no quicker way to end friendships forever.
Moving in together is the most complete and effective way to destroy those bonds and never want to talk to each other much again.
Sure, it works out sometimes.
Ask around. No, it doesn't work out most of the time.

The Kitchen (Chapter 19)

Ya gotta eat.
And eating out is expensive.
Plus, eating noodles every night is a thing, but it sucks.
This is why the kitchen is the most important room in

the house. Yes, there's a strong argument for the bathroom, but don't fight me on this.

KISS: Keep It Simple, Stupid

You don't need a chef's cookware set to cook.
You just need a few good pieces and you'll be gold.

Again, learn to cook and then, learn how to learn more about how to cook. It's not hard. Just learn. Then, do.

First:
Sharp knives are essential. Dull = bad. Sharp = good.
Learn to use a sharp knife. It's not hard. I taught my kids when they were 2. No joke.

Here are the knifes I consider to be the absolute basic "must haves:"
1. paring knife – small and maneuverable
2. long, thin blade knife (about 6")
3. heavy blade chef knife
4. medium ceramic knife
5. vegetable peeler
6. steak knives are optional, but a good idea
7. Bread knife if you bake bread – for obvious reasons

That's it. Those are the basic cutting needs. As you use them, you will learn what each one does best. All you need to sharpen the ceramic one, is a honing steel.
(look it up and look up how to use it)

When you sharpen the others, do NOT use gimmicks or devices.
Get some 120 grit and 300 grit sand paper. (or similar

grits) Learn to sharpen. (look it up) You can certainly get finer grits and go for insanely sharp, but just for daily kitchen use, this will be fine.

Basically you rub the edge of the blade around at a shallow angle on the rougher paper, then do the same on the smoother paper. It's not hard. It will take some practice. And honestly, the honing steel would be a great thing to smooth the edge, and it can be kinda fun. (Yes, there's a whole school of wisdom on knife sharpening, but for basics and beginners, this is a simple way and cost effective way to keep sharp knives.)

You'll want 2 heavy skillets. One large, one smaller. I prefer the ones that are titanium coated. Titanium is bio-compatible. It can't harm you in anyway. And you'll want heavy skillets because the thin ones do not distribute heat very well and can cause uneven cooking results. Plus, thin ones can warp from heating and cooling.
A cast iron skillet. (learn how to use and care for- look it up) This is actually optional in the beginning, but once mastered, it can be one of your best friends.
One small and one medium nonstick pot.
A large nonstick or stainless steal pot.
I highly recommend a pasta pot that has a drain lid. If you don't get one, buy a colander for draining noodles. That's all you need to start. And if you buy good ones that you never abuse, you'll have them for a long time.

Eat on whatever you want. Real dishes or paper. Eventually, you'll learn what kind of dishes you really like. Same with silverware.
If you use real ones, learn how to clean them

completely. I say this for your benefit, not mine.

Learn some basic concepts like browning, searing, saute and broil.
Baking food is generally done at 350° for various amounts of time based on the density and size of the meat. Baking – like cakes and desserts – you should really get a cook book for that. Or look up recipes and FOLLOW THEM.

Seasonings: blends are pretty freaking good and convenient these days. Go with it. But the basics are onion powder, garlic powder, salt, pepper and paprika. I also recommend corriander, cumin, chili powder and sage.
Caution* - read about seasonings. Cayenne powder is good, but can be spicy hot. Always use just a little spice and seasoning, especially when learning. You can always put more in, but ya can't get it out if you use too much!

Oil:

1. peanut for frying
2. olive oil – please spend the $$ on real olive oil. Olive oil can be used in salad dressing or pancakes. It can be used to coat meats to stop sticking and add flavor.
   Add it to pasta to prevent sticking. Add it to pasta with seasoning and eat it! It can even be used as hand lotion.
3. Any other oils, read about what they are best used for and decide if it's in the budget.

Crock pot: Get one. Read the manual. Use it.
You pretty much drop in meat, potatoes, carrots, celery
and seasoning or sauce, turn it on, go to work and
dinner is ready when you get home. Don't forget to add
water before turning it on.

Green things are your friend unless you let it turn green
in the refrigerator. Buy fresh = eat good.

Figure out how to keep your fridge clean, organized and
well stocked.
I don't think a lot of explanation is needed here. Just
discipline.

Do not worry about diets, fats, calories and trendy crap.
The first priority is to stay alive, followed immediately
by stay in relatively decent health.

I'm not a doctor. I'm not a scientist. I'm not a
nutritionist.
But, I am a guy who's been alive long enough to see
things.
I've seen the guy that started the jogging craze for
healthy hearts die of a heart attack. I've seen a world
class trainer and dietitian have a heart attack. I've
watched "them" tell us eggs were good, then bad, then
the best thing on the planet, then terrible again, then
critical to health.
Over and over, I've seen the health experts reverse their
opinions on what is healthy.
Extreme example: Doctors once prescribed smoking,
heroin and cocaine. Then, they realized that wasn't such
a good idea.

I just can't believe it's that complicated.
Animals eat. They survive just fine.
Plants draw nutrients and sit in the sun and survive just fine.
Plants and animals can't drive to the grocery store and pick up a processed pack of anything. They can't microwave a meal. Yet, they survive.

You have it relatively easy. And it's not very complicated.
Humans are omnivores. Eat stuff. Eat a huge variety of stuff.
Don't eat too much. Don't eat too little.
It's not hard.

My strongest guiding principle for eating is this:
I have to eat.
I can only eat so many times a day.
I can only eat so much.
Therefore, if I MUST eat, and I'm limited, I might as well eat the best stuff I can afford that I love to eat.

This is why I learned to be a good cook.

Life as an Adult (Chapter 20)

You have two real options:
1. Live free and wild.
2. Live like a responsible adult.

I assure you that it's not a simple, clear decision.

As an adult, with your own place, you can do anything you want.

The bad news is that you have to pay for everything, and I do mean EVERYTHING you want.

You will want to not do the dishes.

It's not that you won't want to do them. You'll want to <u>not</u> do them. You'll totally understand once you're there.

So, you can live wild and free, eating off of paper plates, staying up and staying out as late as you want. You can eat and drink whatever you want. You can buy whatever you want.

But, you WILL pay for everything.

Living like a responsible adult isn't as bad or boring as it sounds. A little discipline and planning goes a long way. If you use a plate, rinse or wash it as soon as you're done. It takes a few seconds compared to letting it sit and pile up. If you use toilet paper, buy more toilet paper BEFORE you get to the last roll. Again, you'll understand completely when you get there.

It's not hard. It's not complicated.

Learn where the "full line" is on the hamper that matches your washing machine. Do a load when it's full. It's not like you're hauling them to the creek and muscling them over the wash board for an hour. Toss them in with a little – and I emphasize (at this point in history) a little – detergent. Do not pack the washer. Dirty clothes need space for water and detergent to do that voodoo that they do. There has to be enough water to draw the crud from the clothes. Turn the knob and turn it on. Come back later and put the clean, wet

clothes in the dryer. Turn the knob and turn it on. Done. (Side note: If the clothes are dripping wet, something went wrong.
Do NOT put them in the dryer!!!)

Cooking and cleaning are not hard nor complicated. They're not fun. But, they're necessary. And the reward for accomplishing such simple tasks is quite nice. It feels good when someone comes over and they're impressed that you live like a decent human instead of a college frat boy or caveman. A stack of pizza boxes might be funny on the surface, but I guarantee that you're being judged for real.

It seems like a clear, simple, logical decision to live like a decent human in your own dwelling. However, there will be serious temptation to let things go. A couple innocent moments of "get to it later" will pile up before you realize it. Next thing you know, you feel like the place is out of control and a mess. It brings stress and/or a slight depression.

The greatest "secret" to Life as an Adult is that you're never really grown up. You'll never really FEEL like you made it. At least not in the sense of being a fully mature adult. I'm trying to say that you never really feel like a grown up in the way you think of an adult when you're a kid. This needs an illustration.

When I was 23, I had already been through active duty. I had responsibilities that ranged from trivial to monumental. After my Army days, while in college, I was an assistant track coach.

Classes were done for the day. Everyone that was not in spring sports was gone for the day. As I was walking through the halls of the high school towards the track, there were 2 boys messing around in a locker and giggling. Most likely, they were doing something they knew they should not be doing.

They suddenly spotted me moving their way. One of them said in that panicked whisper, "Look out! Here comes an adult!"

I stopped and looked around. I was looking for the adult when I realized that they were talking about **ME**! I was the adult!

I shook my head and said, "Whatever you're doing in that locker, knock it off and go home." They slammed the door shut and scampered away like chipmunks.

I was only 23. And I was suddenly hammered with the slap in the face that I was an adult! How? When? I don't remember taking a test on that! I didn't apply for membership! When I did I become "old?"

Life as an adult can be awesome.
It can be lonely. It can be wild and free. It can be restrictive and costly.
It can be boring. But, ultimately, you get to decide what it can be.

Coworkers & The Work Place (Chapter 21)

I hate to be the one to tell you this, but someone needs to tell you.
And this seems like about as good a spot as any to plop this down.

Never fish from the company pier.
Never fish from the company pond.
Never shit where you eat.

There's probably a dozen ways people will tell you NOT to date your coworkers.
LISTEN TO THEM.
DO NOT DATE YOUR COWORKERS.

I would elaborate, but we've all seen it. People are people and people are dumb. Most end up doing what they feel is right and regret it despite having 100 warnings and dozens of red flags.

I can only tell you that when you date a coworker and it goes bad, you have put yourself in a weak and vulnerable position where they can use soooooo many things against you, including HR.

The work place doesn't have to be boring.
HOWEVER
It's your place of employment. It is not yours. You don't own it. It's not your private playground. Even if you do own it because you own the business, you depend on it for income.
And it's incredibly easy to screw things up for yourself there.

I wish there was a quick and easy cliché for this, but

nope.
Just common sense, common decency and have some dignity and respect. Be responsible. Be professional. Be punctual.
Show up ready to succeed and do the job to the best of your abilities.

Form bonds that allow you to communicate with your coworkers and built trust. The goal is for everyone to pull their weight and do their job. There will ALWAYS be someone that does not. Don't try to "fix them" more than once. Let them reap what they sow. Let them earn whatever they deserve.

Work place politics – it's real. And it will never go away. Why? Because no matter how much employers talk about fairness and bla bla bla.... People are people. They will do what they do.
Someone will always be a brown noser. Someone will always be a snitch. Management will always promote someone that doesn't deserve it. Someone will always try to take credit for your work.
People will get jealous. People will get upset. You'll never really get paid all you feel you're worth and never get enough vacation time.
You're going to have to figure it out. You'll get burned. You'll feel used and lied to. But, you'll see patterns and become wise as serpents.

And never date your coworkers.

Look. Your job at your job is to do your job. That's it.
That doesn't mean to wear blinders and live in a bubble. It means you need to be aware of the fact that you're at

work. It's not a playground. It's not a beauty or popularity contest. It's not a joke, despite the fact that it may feel like one.

Just try to put yourself in a good place for work. Try to make the most of it, because you'll spend a lot of time there. Do everything you can to make the most of it. And do not sabotage yourself at work. Keep your wits = keep your job.

Random Things I Thunk Up (Chapter 22)

Yeah. It's a little silly. But, so am I.
Besides, we all have some random stuff in our heads.

You can't do better or have better if you keep clinging to shit.
Flush the shitty stuff and move on.

Sometimes, you have to say how you feel now matter what it feels like.

The one telling you the rules probably doesn't make the rules.

Once you decide something, don't un-decide. You can listen to reason and make another decision, and explain why you're making another decision, but never second guess yourself. Make the decision, and if you're right, don't back down, even if it means getting your ass handed to you. You will gain respect for standing up to your word. You will never be respected for being spineless.

A towel and a blanket are the same, yet no, they are not.

Crashing waves are seen by surfers as opportunities – not as a destructive, rough sea.

Time is such a bizarre thing.
I don't feel like I have enough of it, yet I have all there is.

The greatest irony about becoming so well connected is just how violently separated we have become.

Some people only have fun by ruining things for others.

People will say things about you.
That's just the way people are.
And they're not generally considerate of what it might mean to you. They may believe that if you're not there to hear it, it doesn't matter.
Do NOT value their words UNLESS you value the person. Even then, consider yourself and your goals and values above all and before all others.
After all – that's how *they* live.

Caution* - I'm not advocating selfishness. I'm not saying to totally disregard others. I AM saying that YOU are the only one that will put yourself and your wants and your needs first. No one else is likely to do that for you. You need to care for you.

If anyone offers to help you for no reason and asking nothing in return, you may want to ask yourself why they're doing it and proceed with caution.

If anyone stops you to ask for directions or assistance or asking for help of any sort, check your surroundings quickly before engaging in any way.
This is the oldest and simplest way for bad people to distract you, get close and do bad things. It's sad that we need to be aware of dangerous people and evil intentions, but it's no joke. We need to be aware of dangerous people and evil intentions. And part of that is to learn how easily they can lure a victim. Sorry for the gloom, but use the knowledge. Ya didn't really believe I was going to go very long without talking about something serious anyways.

On a good note:
There is no logic in fun.
Oh, it has reason and purpose, but not logic.
In fact, we often disregard all safe guards and warnings just to risk everything in order to have a good time.
Even further, the more it feels like we could be seriously hurt or die, the more fun it seems to be.
Getting killed = zero fun.
NEARLY dying while playing around = FUN.

Zero Logic in that, but almost all of our favorite and best stories seem to involve near death experiences. I dunno... Maybe I shouldn't tell younger people that one. Maybe I should admonish them to learn how to have fun after calculating the dangers and risks. Maybe I should encourage them to count the cost before tossing caution to the wind.

In the same breath – you NEED to learn how to have fun

so life doesn't become boring and beat you down. Not having fun is how you end up with depression. Have some fun. Please!

Short Burst (Chapter 23)

Rapid fire truth round

Alcohol is not your friend. It will never do anything good for you, no matter how it feels. There is nothing good at the bottom of a bottle.

You can NOT help someone that does not want to help themselves.
You can NOT save someone that does not want to be saved.
And you just can't save them all.

Everyone who has ever been oppressed, has rebelled. Whether it's a race of people or a teenager with super strict parents. The tighter the grip of authority, the more inevitable the rebellion.

People are cowards.
You will meet some that are brave and courageous. But, as a whole, people are cowards. They will talk about doing stuff, but when it comes time to do stuff, no... they don't.

There's a very thin distinction between brave and crazy. In the military, the difference is shown with a medal.

Very often, help will not appear to be helpful.
You might be annoyed or even angered at someone trying to offer help. The help they're offering may seem futile or inadequate. It's best to try not to be harsh with them. They may actually be helpful, whether it's now or later. It's best not to cause them to never offer to help again.

Some people will bait you into an argument or fight, then blame you for arguing or fighting. They'll pick on you, get in your face and taunt you until you react, they tattle on you and laugh when you get in trouble. These people are human and probably need friends and love and understanding.
But, not from you. Avoid them.

The most adult thing you will ever do is count the cost.
What does that mean?
You do the math BEFORE anything else.
You assess risks and reward, consequences and potential outcomes before you react or respond or anything.

Your kids will drive you nuts. You'll love them anyways.
Other peoples' kids will drive you nuts. You will not.

It's critical to understand an argument before engaging in arguing.

No one has ever changed their mind or view point because of being ridiculed and called names. Well, actually they have, but they did not become a better person. And they definitely never saw things your way. Basic training trainees in the military are the only

exception.
Anyone that has ever been a trainee will get it. Anyone else probably won't.

The government will lie to you. Never trust the government. Ever.

Most people spend 12 years (or so) in public education. Public education is funded and controlled by the government.
That means that the government decides what will be taught and *how* it will be taught, and who will teach it.
Many people go on to state colleges and universities. Again, those are funded and controlled by the government.
Soooooo.......
How can these "free thinkers" that were immersed in government education systems be free thinkers? I'm just askin.

Experts can be wrong. Very wrong.
This does not mean they're wrong all the time.
It does mean that when they are wrong, they are really, really wrong.
And they won't admit it.

Just because someone has been doing something for a long time, that does not mean that they are automatically great at it.

Just because someone has been alive a long time, that does not mean they are wise or respectable.

Just because someone is young, that does not mean

they don't know anything. It does mean that they will have to prove themselves, even if it seems obvious that they know stuff and are clearly right.

People might be impressed with your material possessions.
This does not mean that they like you, respect you or that they think highly of you.

Kindness can be so rare, that it's mistaken for flirting.

Learning about the opposite sex is important. But, real information that matters can be hard to find. And some people (including friends) might make fun of you for trying. It's worth trying.

Getting louder will not win an argument. It will only create a cold wall of resentment. The same goes for name calling.

Honest conversation and civilized debates will generally result in understanding and/or compromise that's reasonable. It takes much longer than name calling or yelling, but the reward is much greater.

This is actually really important. I probably should have started the book with it. But here ya go:
It takes a long time to build a bridge.
It takes much longer than the obvious construction.
It took a lot of people a long time to learn how to do all the things that are necessary to build a reliable bridge that will last. Ground surveyors had to come figure out if the earth would hold a bridge in that spot.
Architects drew plans and engineers provided load

calculations and smart people figured out geometry and structure and on and on.

Planners figured out logistics for materials. Operators prepared the machines and safety protocols. And many more people were involved and ALL of them had to go to school and learn how to do what they do.

Then...

Any idiot with a grenade can walk right up, strap it to the bridge and ruin it in a matter of seconds.

This is what happens when you're trying to make a sane and intelligent argument for something important and someone with a confused or blank look says, "That's stupid." And they just walk away.

It takes a long time and intelligence to make a sound argument or explanation (meaning to build a bridge). It only takes a few seconds of ignorance to shoot it down and destroy everything.

The hardest part of dealing with people – is people.

The trips to see amazing things will be worth it.

The money for amazing food will be worth it.

The time invested in amazing people will be more than worth it.

The time invested in becoming an amazing person will be the best investment you could possibly ever make.

"Be wise as serpents, but gentle as doves" is a Biblical

phrase that will make more sense and become a valuable approach to dealing with people the more you deal with people.

Always remember and never forget:
You are probably more ok than you know. Even when things are really bad.

Sometimes the best thing you can do to help someone is just listen. Offer no advice. Ask only a couple questions. Just be there.

We are not promised anything good in life. We're not actually promised anything at all. The Declaration of Independence says "We hold these truths to be self evident, that all men are created equal, that they are endowed by their Creator with certain unalienable Rights, that among these are Life, Liberty and the pursuit of Happiness."
Most of us have probably heard this part.

Few know the part which is the last line:
"And for the support of this Declaration, with a firm reliance on the protection of divine Providence, we mutually pledge to each other our Lives, our Fortunes, and our sacred Honor."
The guys who wrote this counted the cost.

You have the right to Life, Freedom and the *opportunity to seek joy* in your life. It's up to you to make the most of it. You might even have to risk everything for it. Because it's simply your right. It's not a promise, and it's certainly not provided.

The Most Important Things for Living in America
(Chapter 24)

Pay your Taxes.
The Government has no mercy, and all the time in the world.

Avoid loans for College.
You'll never pay them off, you'll pay an INSANE amount of interest, and if life takes a bad turn, you can NEVER discharge or get rid of them.

Your credit score is more important than your name. While this could change, I highly doubt it. There's too much money in it.

Speaking of crap tons of money...
If a company has lots of advertisements, they are TAKING in lots of money. If you are paying lots of money and receive no tangible assets (think insurance where you don't buy anything, but you pay all the time), then there's a LOT of money to be made in that industry.

Anything expensive: house, car, etc.
Learn as much as you can about it.
Learn how parts of it work so that WHEN something breaks or goes bad, you understand what happened and how much it might cost to fix or replace. If you DON'T know anything about these things and how they work and what's normal or right, you can easily be taken advantage of. There are people and companies that will sell you something you don't need or replace something

that's not actually broken just so they can make money off of you or get more money out of you.

Example: If you have a well and there's no water, it might be the pressure sensor. That's much less money to replace that the pump which is down inside the well. If you don't know the difference or you don't know to ask for them to check that sensor first, you may pay $1,500 instead of just $250.

Reputation is gold.
This is true for yourself as well as for anyone you hire to fix, repair or replace anything you own. A mechanic that has a solid reputation is worth the price over someone cheap that you don't know.
A handyman needs to have a proven track record just like any construction company.

Even if the only thing you ever learn to grow and take care of is just enough to make one fresh batch of salsa every summer, learn. This skill is invaluable and the reward of success can't be measured. It may be a couple plants on a window ledge. Grow something edible – besides weed.

Where you choose to live once you reach adulthood, will affect EVERYTHING... taxes, school quality, crime rate, weather and mood and transportation and quality of life.
These things are not insignificant. Research places. Check the history and look at the businesses, industries and economy for future stability and growth. There are dozens of towns that *WERE* once amazing, then became toilets when things changed. So, no matter where you

call home, ALWAYS have an exit strategy. Even if that means moving back to the parents' house for a couple months. Always, always, always, have money and a plan to move IF the economy of the area tanks.
Do NOT wait to see if gets bad. When it crumbles, go.

Pets/Animals
It's a trade off. And there's too many variables to begin listing, so here's a simple summary.
Just like a house, whatever you own, owns you.
Having a pet can bring you joy and love and stress relief. In the same breath it will bring you frustration, aggravation and stress.
It can also be super expensive, time consuming, messy and, oh yeah... expensive. It's not hard to research and ask around. I know people take their dogs with them to some places while some places won't allow dogs. I know people take their horses on vacation to ride in amazing places. Just do some research and planning before getting ANY animal. Please. It's for YOUR sake AND theirs.

Prepare.
Prepare yourself.
Prepare yourself for situations you might find yourself in.
Prepare yourself to be the kind of person that can have a real and stable relationship.
Prepare yourself to find the same kind of person and be prepared to identify the traits necessary for successful relationships.
Be prepared to walk away.
Prepare yourself to say no in all kinds of times and situations.

Prepare for people to be mean and say bad things when you don't bend over backwards and move mountains for them.

Be prepared to be disappointed.

Prepare your heart and mind for the good and bad, because both will come and both will hit hard.

Be prepared to be flexible without compromising your morals and ethics.

Be prepared to give more than you receive.

Prepare to be the one that stands up when it's time to take a stand. Pray you never have to.

Prepare to be the only one standing when everyone knows what has to be done, but they're too scared to even say anything.

Be prepared to take charge, but don't seek to take charge. You'll know when it's the right thing to do.

Be prepared to let people learn the hard way. You can only help or save them so long.

Prepare for war and famine, but enjoy peace and prosperity.

Prepare to win. Be prepared to lose.

Prepare to live.

Be prepared to die.

This is where you will find true peace. Because you will be prepared for all things knowing you can welcome anything life may bring... or take.

Summary (Chapter 25)

The cruelest irony of being a parent is that we do everything possible to prevent the next generation from suffering the hard lessons we learned, only to have our experience and all we know scoffed, dismissed and mocked. They tell us we're too old to understand. They tell us that we just don't understand the younger generation. They think we don't care what they feel or how they think.

Bullshit.

We totally understand! We lived it! We survived it! We know where the traps are – LISTEN TO US!!!

Women make fun of men for throwing away the instructions on how to assemble new toys and furniture. Well, guess what. Each generation does that exact thing. The old folks have the road map. They made the map. Each new generation crumples it up, burns it and then drives off into the field or wilderness with no map.

The part I can't figure out is why.
Why do we honestly, whole heartedly believe that we have infinitely more understanding in our 16 years of existence than those that have been here 4 decades longer than us?
How does this world infect the young minds so well?

I'll admit that when I was 16, I wondered why anyone would even WANT to live past 30. They were so dead inside. They acted like they didn't care about the world or even their own life. They had no dreams. They had no ambition to change this world for the better. They just went to their dead end jobs every day and did the same lame stuff every evening and weekend. I didn't see them learning new stuff or trying to become better at anything. I was convinced that there was no real life after 30. "Old People" were dead. They were just zombies.

I'm telling you, I knew everything when I was 16! HaHa! Right?

At the time of writing this book, I was 56 years old - well past my "usefulness." And all the amazing things I'm experiencing now would take a whole book to explain. I can only say that I have a whole new and exciting life ahead of me, and I greet it with open arms and wonder.

But I still wonder what makes us think we know everything when we're 16. Is it genetic? Is it taught? Is it osmosis from media and government?

We had no idea how much we didn't know, but thought we knew it all.

Then, as we aged, we found out.

I think it's just a flaw in being human.

They say that when you die, you don't know you're dead, so it doesn't bother you. But, it affects those around you tremendously. The same thing happens when you're stupid.

Perhaps, when we're young, we FEEL like we've learned a massive amount of information. But, we lack the experience to realize that we only know what we've been taught SO FAR. Always remember and never forget: there is no substitute for experience.

And when you're young, you just don't have enough life experience to know certain things. (That's a very long and windy rabbit trail if ya wanna take it.) In fact, I'll say it again: You can't possibly know how much you don't know.

Simple example for those that have traveled to the edge of the Grand Canyon - You saw pictures, read books and watched movies with the Grand Canyon described. But, nothing compared to being there. Nothing gave you the sense and smell and impact that being there gave you.

Another simple illustration: Even something as simple and common as fresh baked cookies or a holiday dinner - pictures and descriptions don't compare to getting that big whiff of delicious. If you can close your eyes and "almost smell it" that's because you've experienced it. There's no substitute for experience.

Explaining life it is not hard or complicated. But, yes it is. It takes time.
Ya can't explain or teach everything about math in 3 days. It takes time. And effort. And so does life.

Understanding life? That's the magic sauce.
The simple truth of youthful arrogance is that there's no way to know how much we don't know. It's like we piled snow up high enough to sled ride down and thought we reached some level of achievement because we had never been to a real hill. Then, we get to a hill and think we're "way up there," because we had never been to a real mountain. Once we see the mountains, we finally start to understand that we don't really know what "way up there" is.

It's not until we understand how much we don't understand that we finally get it. Once our eyes open to the truth about how much knowledge and understanding we still haven't even seen, we can finally become mature.

So, for all of us that are living... just buckle up!
It's gonna be one hell of a ride.
You have sooooo much more to learn no matter what age you are!!
I wish there was some magic dust I could sprinkle on you to make everything perfect.
But, I can only hope this helps a tiny bit.
Take care and take time to.

The End

Written and edited by Jozef Kojs

Cover art by Jozef Kojs

Audiobook version read and recorded by Jozef Kojs

To clayton

love Joe

Made in the USA
Monee, IL
11 June 2023